WHEN
VIOLENCE
IS THE
ANSWER

ALSO BY TIM LARKIN

Survive the Unthinkable

How to Survive the Most Critical 5 Seconds of Your Life

WHEN VIOLENCE IS THE ANSWER

Learning How
to Do What It Takes
When Your Life Is at Stake

TIM LARKIN

LITTLE, BROWN AND COMPANY

New York Boston London

Hachette Book Group supports the right to free expression and the value of copyright. The purpose of copyright is to encourage writers and artists to produce the creative works that enrich our culture.

The scanning, uploading, and distribution of this book without permission is a theft of the author's intellectual property. If you would like permission to use material from the book (other than for review purposes), please contact permissions@hbgusa.com. Thank you for your support of the author's rights.

Little, Brown and Company
Hachette Book Group
1290 Avenue of the Americas, New York, NY 10104
littlebrown.com

First Edition: September 2017

Little, Brown and Company is a division of Hachette Book Group, Inc. The Little, Brown name and logo are trademarks of Hachette Book Group, Inc.

The publisher is not responsible for websites (or their content) that are not owned by the publisher.

The Hachette Speakers Bureau provides a wide range of authors for speaking events. To find out more, go to hachettespeakersbureau.com or call (866) 376-6591.

ISBN 978-0-316-35464-6
Library of Congress Control Number: 2017943271

10 9 8 7 6 5 4 3 2 1

LSC-C

Printed in the United States of America

To my many friends working in the shadows. Quiet professionals who shun publicity and do the real work of protecting our freedom so we may live our lives without having to deal with the many asocial predators who would gladly take it from us. They can't get them all, but you'd be amazed at how many they quietly hunted down without fanfare. Their reward is doing the job, and I'm proud to call these operators my friends.

CONTENTS

WHEN
VIOLENCE
IS THE
ANSWER

IN THE BEGINNING

Violence is rarely the answer, but when it is, it's the *only* answer.

As a society, we have focused nearly all our energy on the first part of that statement. We don't just want to believe that violence is rarely the answer—we want to believe it is *never* the answer—and so in recent years we have set out to identify every instance where that is true. Admittedly, there are many of them, and we have gotten very good at describing them to anyone who will listen. As good as we've become at advocating nonviolence, we have gotten even better at dismissing those rare instances where violence actually *is* the only answer. We put asterisks next to those events and pigeonhole them as the exclusive domain of criminals and cops. We have not only convinced ourselves that this vision of the world is real, but we have taught it to our children as gospel by building layers of protection and insulation around them to reinforce the truthfulness of our vision. Unfortunately, we are not seeing straight. We have created a society where the blind are leading the blind.

My goal with this book is to open your eyes.

I am a violence expert. I know what violence is, how it

works, how to use it, and how to avoid it. As an expert in the field of life-and-death self-defense for the last twenty-five years, I have counseled, trained, and taught tens of thousands of men and women across the globe. Rich and poor, big and small, frail and strong, military and civilian—I've seen them all. Each of my students has a different story, but 70 percent of them have something in common: they only sought out help *after* surviving an act of violence.

Seventy percent.

Think about that number for a second. In a training class of twenty people, that means fourteen have endured the physical and emotional trauma of violence. Fourteen of them are victims. The other six probably know someone who recently became a victim and it jarred them into action.

It's relatively rare in my business to have a student who doesn't have a story to tell, who is being proactive and wants to be prepared. The rarity of this occurrence is both one of the most frustrating parts of my job and the most understandable. Who really wants to think about this stuff if they don't have to? A bigger, stronger, faster person, intent on doing you grievous bodily harm, is a base fear of every human. It's only natural to try to push those fears out of our minds when we lack the skills and the knowledge to act effectively in defense of ourselves and our loved ones. Instead, we hope our fears are never realized and we try to rationalize them away: "I don't need to worry about this. I live in the right neighborhood. I have the right friends. I am a good person. Stuff like this doesn't happen to people like me." I'm sorry, but you're wrong.

Aside from how dangerous these cavalier attitudes are (for reasons I will explain in depth later), hoping or rationalizing does little to actually reduce your fear. Wishful thinking only compartmentalizes and suppresses it, and only briefly. If you're a woman, maybe the fear erupts to the surface when an unfamiliar man walks into the parking garage elevator with you. If you're a man, maybe it creeps in when a friend of a friend is particularly aggressive with you in a social situation. The question you need to ask yourself in a situation like that is, "What is at the bottom of this fear?"

In my experience, the essence of that fear is that if someone becomes a physical threat—especially if they appear to be bigger, stronger, and faster than you—you have nothing in your toolbox to deal with it. You are helpless and vulnerable. You are in trouble.

With this book, I hope to change that sense of helplessness and vulnerability. Thankfully, for most of us, violence is an anomaly—a black swan event whose likelihood is as predictable as its consequences, which is to say *not very.* Most people will go their entire lives without experiencing serious violence. But those who do will feel firsthand its power to drastically change, or even end, lives. It only has to happen once.

I know it's uncomfortable to think about a moment like this. But you have to come to terms with the fact that someday, somebody might try to physically control or attack you. It's perfectly within the range of possibilities for our lives, as it has been for the entire history of human civilization. Just ask every real victim of violence that I have worked with or trained.

When it comes to other rare events that can have destructive consequences on our lives, we aren't shy about preparing for them. We have fire extinguishers, disaster preparedness kits, car insurance, health insurance, flood insurance, and life insurance because we know there are things in this world outside of our control, and being prepared for them gives us confidence that we will be able to get through them if and when they arrive.

So why do so few of us have a plan for unexpected violence? For some reason, we see training for self-defense as a Herculean effort reserved for the physically elite, so we dismiss it. That means there are just two main groups who study and prepare for violence. One group is the predators (we'll talk more about them later). The other group is the professional protectors, like the police and military. Many people are content to bank on those protectors to be there in times of need. But pinning all your hopes on the possibility that one of those professionals will be on the very spot at the very moment you're in danger is a lot like throwing out your fire extinguisher in the hopes that a fire truck will be turning the corner onto your block the very moment the flames touch the drapes.

I don't want to live like that, and this book is for those who don't want to live like that, either.

Obviously, I hope violence never visits you. But we don't always control whether we experience violence. That's never entirely up to us, because violence is an equal opportunity offender. It cuts across all demographic lines—race, gender, sexual orientation, religion, nationality, socioeconomic status. There is no amount of privilege or social standing that can make you immune to, or allow you to opt out of, violence when someone has identified you as their target. The choice you do have is whether you're going to be ready for it. I believe that the wisest thing we can do is ready ourselves for the kind of moment we hope never happens. The solution to fear is not denial and wishful thinking; it is knowledge, preparedness, and confidence.

My goal with this book is to arm you with all three of those virtues by changing the way you think about the subject of violence. I want you to be one of those six people in my class who are willing to learn from the misfortune of others not because you *want* to, but because you *need* to. Knowing what violence is, preparing your mind for what is necessary to either avoid or deploy it, and developing the confidence that you can get it done when it counts are life skills we've all been ignoring for decades. It's time for that to change.

MY CAREER AS A NAVY SEAL ENDED BEFORE IT STARTED

I grew up with dreams of invincibility. For as long as I can remember as a Navy brat, I wanted to be a frogman, better known today as a member of the Navy SEAL teams. Just before high school, my family moved to Coronado, California, where the SEALs have their training base, and we lived in Navy housing directly across from their infamous obstacle course. I remember watching in awe as guys navigated the course. I couldn't believe there was a job out there where you got paid to work out, hang out at the beach, dive, shoot automatic weapons, jump out of airplanes, and just blow stuff up.

I spent the next ten years learning everything there was to know about the Navy SEALs. By the time I finished high school, I knew everything about SEAL training. I knew about how to prepare for it, I knew where to hide food during training, I knew which teams to go to. In college at the University of Southern California, I did Navy ROTC and worked my tail off. When I graduated, entered the Navy, and got selected to Basic Underwater Demolition/SEAL (BUD/S) training, I had become exactly the kind of guy I just warned you about—I was bigger, faster, and stronger than all my peers. I was a machine. And with the Navy's help, I would become a *killing* machine.

I was tenacious. I led my boat crew to successful evolutions time and time again during the first phase of training. We even won Hell Week—the five-day gauntlet of exhausting, sleepless, physical and mental punishment they put you through at the end of the first phase to cull the herd. I flew through every aspect of SEAL training after that. I was inarguably the top guy in my class. We started with about eighty men and not one of them could touch me.

About two weeks prior to graduation, in the last phase of training, we were on a very basic dive mission; our task was to practice tying explosives to a submerged object. I had a minor sinus infection that day, but I didn't think much of it, so I dove in without a second thought. I felt the pressure against my ears but forced myself to continue deeper into the cold Pacific Ocean waters to complete the evolution. Everything was going fine—I was swimming well, I found the obstacle—but as I was mounting the explosives, an underwater wave hit the side of my head. (There are waves underwater, just like the ones on the surface). The wave had enough force, combined with the pressure already exerting itself against my body, to burst my eardrum. I felt a shock of cold surge up through my head, like ice water shooting directly into my brain. Then I felt warm liquid leaking out of my semicircular canal. As soon as that warm liquid oozed out, I went into vertigo and lost all sense of balance. I had no idea which way was up. The only thing that saved me was the guide-rope attached to the inflatable boat on the surface above me. I was able to pull myself up the rope, but just barely. The whole time it felt like I was pulling myself at a forty-five-degree angle toward the bottom.

When I broke the surface, my head was slapping against the water uncontrollably and a couple of the instructors struggled to pull me into the boat. Blood was pouring out of my ears, and I was shaking violently. They quickly assessed my situation and I stabilized before even getting to shore. But when the Navy doctors examined my ear, less than half an hour after the initial trauma, they told me that it would never fully heal and I knew my career as a SEAL was over. It was never going to happen.

It ended up being a turning point in my life. It was my first experience with real injury. I had been hit hard and knocked down, I'd sprained and twisted things, I'd been *hurt,* but I'd never been fully incapacitated by physical injury. I had trained my whole life to be bigger, faster, and stronger than anyone I encountered—to be invincible—yet none of that could help me when this tiny membrane I couldn't see was ruptured by a wave of pressure I couldn't see coming, and it left me with no control over my body. Almost immediately I had a profound realization about the power of injury. A tiny change in pressure from an unexpected opponent had stopped me cold. This insight—though I didn't fully understand it at the time—would guide the rest of my career and, as it happens, become a central premise of this book.

PUBLIC SERVICE TO PRIVATE SECTOR

After I recovered from my accident, I moved into special operations intelligence at the Naval Special Warfare Command until I got out of the Navy in 1991, right after the U.S. invasion of Panama. At the same time, my experience with injury led me to learn everything I could about trauma to the human body—how it works, how to inflict it, and how to avoid it. At the time, the lion's share of self-defense instruction and hand-to-hand combat tactics—both in the civilian sector and in the military—were designed around defending against or exploiting the differences in human beings. But the injury that caused me to lose my career as a SEAL helped me to understand that there might be a better approach: focusing on the weaknesses that all human bodies share. After all, certain areas of the body are always vulnerable, regardless of size, speed, and strength. I was living proof of that.

Perhaps my most influential teacher about the weak points in the human body was an expert on hand-to-hand combat and special warfare, named "P.J.," who'd found a niche in the private sector after it got out that he was training SEALs in hand-to-hand combat. When I completed my active duty service, P.J. asked me to help him train several large corporate clients whose security personnel wanted to know everything P.J. was teaching the SEALs. I had decided to take six months off after getting out of the Navy, so I said yes. That six-month break quickly turned into a decade of training Fortune 100 companies, international aid agencies, and NATO military detachments all over the world. It was probably one of the most exciting, eye-opening times in my life.

P.J.'s training concept was deceptively simple: because the body follows the mind, effective combat is all about shutting down your opponent's most valuable weapon—his brain. A debilitating injury to the body takes the brain out of the equation and destroys any strength, speed, or size advantage the opponent might have. My diving incident was a perfect example. It didn't matter that I was strong: the injury to my inner ear destroyed my sense of balance and orientation, and forced my brain to deal with the acute trauma to my body at the expense of engaging the body parts I wanted to control both to complete the dive evolution and swim to the surface. I was completely helpless and vulnerable. And if someone like me, who is not just bigger, faster, and stronger, but also tenacious and fiercely mission-focused, can be laid low by injury, so, too, can others who seem to benefit from all possible advantages.

That was very much the foundation of a weekend training seminar I ran for a group of investment bankers in New York City, all of whom traveled extensively overseas. They were most concerned about the risks of international air travel and what they could do to defend themselves against attackers who would almost certainly be armed. I showed them what could be legally taken on an airplane—by them or by hijackers—including scissors and box cutters. This seminar took place on September 8th and 9th, 2001. We videotaped the whole thing for other members of the group who couldn't attend. I flew home to Vegas Monday evening, September 10th. We all know what happened the next morning.

The tapes from those training sessions—which took place at a facility destroyed by debris from the collapse of the World Trade Center towers—marked the beginning of my work in self-defense instruction as the sole focus of my career. The lessons contained within those tapes became the foundation of my study of violence, which began in earnest that day.

HOW THIS BOOK WORKS

In the following chapters, I am going to talk to you about violence. I am going to tell you stories about a select few of my students and clients—some who knew what it took to survive when their lives were at stake, others who sadly did not. I am going to teach you what I taught them: the principles of violence.

I am going to put in front of you the evidence and the data that back it all up. Together we will examine some uncomfortable truths and attempt to destigmatize and demystify some popular misconceptions about self-protection. My goal is to get you to change the way you think about violence, so that you might fully understand it and finally free yourself from the prison of helplessness and vulnerability. By the end of this book, you will have the knowledge you need to minimize the potential for violence in your life, be prepared to deal with violence when it enters your life, and have the confidence that you will be successful when it matters most.

While I will teach you how to think about training,* this isn't a step-by-step, "punch here, kick there" encyclopedia of training techniques. This book is about stamping the princi-

---

* Free supplemental video training content is also available online.

ples of violence into your subconscious. It's about turning your brain into the ultimate concealed carry.

In my years of studying this material, I've come to understand one central truth that sits at the core of self-protection and thus will sit at the core of my approach to this book:

Techniques get you killed. Principles save your life.

It's like that old saying: give a man a fish and he will eat for a day, teach him how to fish and he will eat for a lifetime. The same is true of self-protection. Teaching you a few techniques in this book will only help you in a few scenarios. But if I teach you the principles of self-protection, and change the way you think about violence, you'll be able to handle any scenario without hesitation.

Thus, I've organized the book into ten chapters that examine violence in the modern world and teach you what you need to know to live comfortably, confidently, and securely in that world.

There are two parts, each containing five chapters:

Part 1: How to Think About Violence — is about accepting some unpleasant truths about the nature of violence in self-protection, while developing the mindset and intent necessary to engage with violence in time to, one day, save your life. You know how they tell addicts that the first step to dealing with an addiction is admitting you have one? Violence is the same way. That's why it's important that these ideas kick off the book.

Part 2: How to Think About *Using* Violence — is about the principles of training you need to understand to evaluate and engage the training modalities best suited for you. These are the fundamental physical principles necessary to prepare yourself for the worst and execute an effective plan of action under pressure.

The concepts in this book will lay a critical foundation for correctly processing and performing the mental and physical elements of self-protection. Understanding the methodologies and principles behind violence is the only way to properly employ it in a real-life situation. As you read on, you might feel like you're jumping into the ocean for the first time, but you'll soon adjust and easily keep your head above water. To be clear, getting comfortable with the subject matter doesn't make you one of "them"—one of those asocial psychopaths who traffic in indiscriminate violence. I talked to many of them in the research for this book. I promise, you're not them. And I promise that I am not an advocate of violence for violence's sake, no matter how chilling or upsetting you find some of the language you are about to read. I truly believe that violence is almost never the answer. But when it is, it is the only answer, and we all need to be prepared for it.

A NOTE BEFORE WE BEGIN

Throughout this book, I will be leaning on the masculine pronouns—he, him, his—when I am not telling a specific story. This is not out of disrespect for the fighting capacity of women or disregard for the frightening degree to which they are victims of certain violent crimes. Many of my best, most dedicated, and courageous clients are women, and everything in this book applies to them equally. I've made this choice because men are disproportionately responsible for the asocial violent crime committed in our society as well as the many mistakes made in instances of social aggression that lead to grave bodily injury and death. I am using the male pronouns because men are the ones who need to be talked to directly, over and over again, for the lessons to get past the ego defenses.

Okay, let's jump in!

PART 1

HOW TO THINK ABOUT VIOLENCE

CHAPTER ONE

VIOLENCE IS A TOOL

Our Age of Anxiety is, in great part, the result of trying to do today's job with yesterday's tools and yesterday's concepts.

—*Marshall McLuhan*

As a society, we struggle to distinguish between violence and the people who use it. Since we mostly associate violence with criminals, we tell ourselves that violence itself is criminal, violence is evil, violence is *bad*. We think that because violence is undesirable, to study it is to endorse it—to say that we think it is *desirable*. There is a certain logic to this point of view at the surface. If criminals do something often enough, that something is probably going to be criminal itself. The problem with that logic, however, is that it conflates the means with the ends. Because we are so uncomfortable with violence, we have convinced ourselves subconsciously that the "what" and the "why" are the same things: in other words, we tell ourselves that, because criminals often use violence, violence itself is always criminal. But that's a big mistake: violence is a tool like any other. As with any other tool, the proper object of our moral and ethical judgment isn't the "what"—after all, you wouldn't call a screwdriver or a toothbrush evil—but rather the "why," the ends to which human beings choose to direct it.

I want to take you through a hypothetical scenario to make this point a little less abstract. I've posed this thought exercise to thousands of new students and seminar attendees over the years. It's about a woman I'm calling Diane and it is an amalgamation of several real-life stories.

It was supposed to be an ordinary night for Diane. Her husband was away on business and she had no other plans, so she chopped up a salad for dinner, put the baby to bed, took out the trash, then turned on the TV in the kitchen while she washed the dishes.

Unfortunately, she forgot to lock the back door.

As she casually scrubbed a plate with one eye on a Law & Order *rerun that she'd seen a hundred times, the kitchen door swung open behind her. Before she could turn around, a pair of massive hands grabbed her and forced her up against the kitchen counter.*

These were definitely not her husband's hands.

She tried to scream, but it was too late. The intruder covered her mouth and reached for the drawstrings on her sweats. She struggled and squirmed, but his grip, even with one arm, was too much for her. Scared for her life, Diane's mind suddenly flashed to the baby upstairs. She had to do something.

In desperation, she reached back and clawed at the man's face, digging her nails deeply into his skin. She hoped it would force him to let go of her and she could run and scream for help. The intruder let out a horrible howl as blood streamed down his face, but he didn't let up. Instead, he got angry. He grabbed the chef's knife still sitting out on the cutting board and plunged it into the side of Diane's neck.

Her eyes rolled back. It was over in seconds.

———

This story is very disturbing. But alongside the reflexive pain we feel when we hear this story is a deep anger when we think about the man—*the murderer*—who destroyed this family. For him, any semblance of sympathy quickly disappears. This man should never see the light of day again. At a minimum, he should be incarcerated for the rest of his life. It is an understandable and entirely justifiable reaction—legally and morally.

Now let's rewind to the moment Diane is at the sink washing the dishes and watching TV. I want to tell you this part of the story again, but with a twist...

———

...the kitchen door swung open behind her. Before she could turn around, a pair of massive hands grabbed her and forced her up against the kitchen counter.

These were definitely not her husband's hands.

As she was thrown up against the kitchen counter, Diane immediately sensed that the man attacking her was bigger, faster, and stronger than she was. This triggered a pair of realizations in her mind: 1) If she tried only to scream or scratch her way out of his grasp, nothing good was likely to come of it, and 2) If she had any hopes to escape, she would have to inflict serious injury on this man.

In desperation, she looked around for something to grab—anything with some weight or an edge. She saw the chef's knife she'd used to make her salad; it was just within her reach. She grabbed the knife while the man fumbled with her drawstrings and plunged it into the side of his neck.

His eyes rolled back. It was over in seconds.

This version of the story is equally disturbing, and again most of us probably have a very similar response to reading it. In this version of the story, we see a hero. We see a mother who, in a life-or-death situation, acted in self-defense to protect not only herself, but her infant child. She should face no legal consequences, right? In fact, she should be lauded, protected to the full extent of the law, and held up as a shining example of someone who courageously fought off a violent criminal to save herself and her family.

But, wait. Violence is evil. Violence is a crime. Only criminals use violence, remember? Doesn't that make Diane a bad person? A criminal? That's how the logic of our normal mental model for violence is supposed to work. *Sure,* you're probably thinking to yourself, *but this is different.*

That is exactly my point.

Sadly, the first version of that story is much more common than the second. When we hear stories about someone being stabbed to death by a stranger, the majority of the time the stabber is the villain and the victim is the innocent. Between 2006 and 2010, for example, the FBI reported more than nine thousand homicides by "knives or cutting instruments" in the United States, yet only three were deemed legally justifiable.* That's because, like in the first version of our story, there is almost always a crucial asymmetry between the perpetrator and the victim in the application of violence: only the story's villain was willing to inflict injury, even to kill, and so the villain won.

But along with the differences between the two scenarios, there is also one key similarity: *The knife to the side of the neck worked the same each time.*

In the first case, the knife ended the life of an innocent person. In the second case, it saved the life of a woman and her child. But it was the same knife. It worked in the hands of the "good guy" the same way it worked in the hands of the "bad guy."

That knife is just a tool. It has no moral compass or intention. It does not pick sides. It does whatever the person wielding it wants it to do, for whatever reason they want to do it. It can be used for evil or for good, to destroy or to protect. Diane's attacker used a kitchen knife to end her life. Diane used it to save her life. But the only thing we can truly judge about the knife itself is whether it worked.

There is a broad spectrum of purposes and intentions for most tools. Awareness of that fact is what is often missing when we think about violence. Its absence leaves us with tunnel vision, it renders us unprepared and ill-informed, and it prevents us from evaluating this admittedly uncomfortable subject for what it truly is. This is a clinical, dispassionate way

---

* https://ucr.fbi.gov/crime-in-the-u.s/2010/crime-in-the-u.s.-2010/tables/10shrtbl08.xls, https://ucr.fbi.gov/crime-in-the-u.s/2010/crime-in-the-u.s.-2010/tables/10shrtbl14.xls

to look at the subject of violence, I know, but when it comes to moments of life or death, if you enjoy being alive, all that is going to matter is that whatever you did to save your life actually worked. Ninety-nine times out of one hundred, the answer will not be violence. It will be avoidance or de-escalation. But that one time when violence is the answer, make no mistake, it will be the only answer.

That is what you need to understand when your life is at stake, and it starts with the sober recognition that violence is not an ideal, or a way of life, or a value—it's a tool, plain and simple.

Sure, even in the first story Diane tried to defend herself, by instinctively scratching and clawing. But it wasn't enough: one person was engaging in real, serious violence, and the other was only reacting to it. The person who merely reacts to violence—who is unwilling to meet their assailant on an even playing field when their own safety demands it—is always at a disadvantage. Perhaps you want self-protection to be a sanitized form of violence, one that doesn't hurt quite as much. Sorry to say, there's no such thing. A knife wound inflicted in an act of self-defense looks just like a knife wound inflicted in an act of murder. Violence is violence.

What that means is, we need to think about scenarios of violence not from the perspective of the victim, but of the *winner*—even when the victim is the "good guy" and the winner is a criminal. Of course, we can do that without condoning unprovoked violence or sympathizing with the criminal; we're not thinking morally here, but tactically. And tactically speaking, we need to answer some key questions about every violent encounter: When did everything shift to favor one person over the other? When did they get a result with the tool of violence? How did they get that result? Is it something that can be replicated by anyone on a regular basis?

Again, these aren't moral questions. Everything that happens prior to violence has a separate set of rules, many of which have to do with defusing dangerous situations before violence breaks out. Before violence, we can practice anger management, meditation, or simply the habit of walking away when situations get too heated. Similarly, everything that happens *after* an act of violence is handled by our justice system. That's when we start using words like "self-defense" or "murder" (which are technical terms with very specific legal definitions). There are reams of books on either side of the discrete points of violence, but very few on the act itself. This book focuses on the moments when violence is actually happening. That narrow window of time where we, as sane, socialized citizens, would be justified in using the tool in defense of self or others. My message is a simple one: to avoid being a victim of violence, you need to learn from it.

LEARNING FROM VIOLENCE

Have you ever heard of "the knockout game"? Here's how it's supposed to work: An unsuspecting citizen walks down the street, going about their day, when one of a group of (typically) young males points them out and challenges a friend to sneak up on that person and knock them out with a single sucker punch. A few years ago, stories of marauding groups of young men playing this game flooded in from across the United States and, in a few cases, even Europe.

It was violence at its most random.

Chances are, if you heard about the knockout game, it was from a news broadcast or an article on one of your social media channels. The commentary was probably breathless and frightening, and if you are like many of my first-time seminar attendees, you mentally braced yourself to shake it off as you turned up the volume or clicked the link: *This is too unpleasant to think about. It's just an urban legend,* you yourself. *If those people really were attacked, there had to have been a reason for it.*

How you react to this kind of news matters, because our instinct is to focus our attention on the types of violent encounters that feel like they have an explanation—rape is about sex, robbery is about property, bar fights are about social hierarchy, murder is about vengeance, etc. These acts make sense to us, so we can envision scenarios for avoiding, protecting, and defending ourselves from them. The same cannot be said for an act of pure, inexplicable violence like the knockout game. We can pretend like it doesn't exist, but that's not only impractical, it's imperiling. It won't protect you, and it will never make you safer.

Still, our instinct with something like the knockout game far too often is to avert our gaze from the grisly details and to distance ourselves from the kind of people who play it. I understand this mindset. Life is already complicated enough, we shouldn't have to wrestle with the reality that we live in a world where kids can attack you in the street for the thrill of it. It's a perfectly comprehensible modern, gut response—but a dangerous one just the same. Because the people who play the knockout game are the only ones who can teach us anything about how not to lose at it. When we say, "Geez, I hope that never happens to me," all we're doing is closing ourselves off to learning while giving the perpetrator super-powers in our minds—as if the only thing that can protect us is hoping and praying.

When we ask, "Why did that work?", on the other hand, those super-powers start to dissolve as we begin to empower ourselves with the knowledge that we possess the same basic ability. There's nothing magical about clocking an unsuspecting stranger in the head—each of us could do it today. We won't, of course, but understanding how this kind of raw violence works reminds us that the perpetrators of violence are human, just like we are. It replaces irrational fear with a mindset primed for preparedness, and it can make the key, initial difference in how you stand up to and face down violence should it ever come into your own life.

There is a lot we can learn from random violence if we approach it from an investigative, even clinical perspective, analyzing any violent situation the way a coroner would examine a fatality. A coroner will certainly have compassion for innocent victims of violence—but when it comes time to do her job, she'll put feeling aside and think dispassionately. She'll identify damaged organs and the nature of the damage they sustained. She'll try to understand what happened and how it happened, and she'll do that by breaking down the physics and physiology of the perpetrator's actions. In just the same way, when we hear about victims of random violence, we have to temporarily put aside our compassion for them, and dispassionately ask how the perpetrator came to turn these people into victims and what kind of physical damage they were able to inflict.

The basic idea isn't so different from what I did in military intelligence. We want to learn as much as possible about our enemies. We want to get inside their heads—not because we want to imitate them, or because we are unsympathetic to their victims—but because we want to stay a step ahead of them.

So, what can we learn from something like the knockout game to make its abhorrent existence actually useful to us?

First, that *random violence happens.* We don't need to embrace it, condone it, or even understand what drives it, but we must accept that it is an inevitable part of being alive. *People hurt other people*—physically, sometimes fatally.

Then we can *examine the act from a purely tactical perspective.* The knockout game is an example of indiscriminate, asocial violence. But why does it work? Tactically speaking, it is an attack that utilizes the element of surprise on an unsuspecting, unprepared victim. The inability to anticipate the threat allows the perpetrator to put a well-placed strike into a vulnerable part of the human body resulting in severe injury—usually a concussion, but sometimes death from blunt force trauma if the unconscious victim's head hits the pavement or some other hard surface or sharp edge.

With knowledge of how an attack works we can then *develop avoidance tactics.* If lack of what we called in the military "situational awareness" is a significant factor in acts of random violence like the knockout game, how can we be more alert to make us less ideal targets? How about not walking around with our earbuds in and our heads buried in our phones? Listening to music full blast and staring into the abyss of our never-ending Facebook news feed effectively makes us deaf and blind. In the wild, a deaf and blind animal is the ideal prey for any opportunistic predator. It's no different for the kind of person who would play the knockout game. Anything we can do to be more alert makes us less likely to become a target.

None of these insights are revolutionary. They're common sense. Sitting in the comfort of your home or your subway ride to work, you have the luxury of reading this and saying, "Well, duh!", then turning the page. But is it really that obvious? Have you ever really imagined yourself becoming the victim of random violence? Have you ever come up with a concrete game plan in response, or even ahead of time? Have you ever considered that your best defense against this kind of violence is using it first, and better? (It's not hard—this section just taught you what it takes to knock out a knockout artist)

I can assure you that most people have not. The 70 percent victimization rate across my three decades of first-time students is a testament to that reality. For them, these insights were like learning a new language—the language of violence—and their obviousness only developed in retrospect, after they'd become conversational in the language in which those insights were spoken.

What's interesting, though, is that this language isn't new. In fact, it might be our native tongue. What I mean is, humans as a species are good at using the tool of violence. With opposable thumbs, big brains, forward-set eyes, and strong canine teeth, we have a predator's build. One that makes us hardwired to be good at violence. We can create weapons, work in packs, and manipulate situations. Our ability to think strategically, tactically, and judiciously about violence has been core to our survival as a species from day one. Our brains have made us the smartest species on the planet, and our capacity for compassion has made us the most advanced, but our natural ability for using violence to our advantage has made us truly superior.

You possess that same innate ability to consider, to be comfortable with, to even utilize violence, even if those capabilities are deeply latent. And along with the hardwired ability to inflict violence comes the protective "spidey sense"—the capacity to anticipate violence before it happens—that is also wired into our biology.

In that sense, I am not trying to turn you into someone or something you are not. All I'm trying to do is reactivate that primal ability to defend yourself and protect the ones you love. To do that, we have to look at the tool of violence as straightforwardly as possible, and strip away all the emotion, drama, and social baggage that keeps us from using our prehensile hands to pick it up when we need it most.

THE TRAINED PERSON IS NEVER HARMLESS

I was once hired to give a self-defense presentation to a corporate group aboard a cruise ship. The company had arranged a Caribbean cruise for several of its employees and their families, and my presentation was informally billed as a kind of father-daughter event. One of those women, whom I will call Sara, was the daughter of a man I happened to know fairly well. He told me she was coming with him to the seminar whether she liked it or not, since she was getting ready to go to college. Many of the other daughters came to the seminar under a similar state of silent protest—they wanted to go do other things, like tan or swim or hit the buffet—anything else but this. I understood: it was the Caribbean, after all.

When I met Sara she was a carbon copy of Reese Witherspoon's character in *Legally Blonde*. Bubbly and effervescent, she talked like her, she carried herself like her, she was just *that* girl. Learning about self-defense was clearly not at the top of Sara's list of priorities that afternoon, but to her credit she went through all the training with a standard level of disinterest and did nothing to make the event more difficult (unlike some of the fathers, intent on impressing their daughters). Afterward I didn't think much of our limited exchanges, frankly. It was just another corporate seminar.

Three years later, I was holding a series of seminars in New York City and she walked in with her three younger sisters in tow. "Do you remember me?" she asked. She didn't have quite the same stereotypical "ditzy blonde" affect, but she looked more or less the same.

"Of course I do. Nice to see you again."

"Did Dad call you and tell you what happened?"

"No," I said, "what happened?"

Soon after the cruise, Sara moved into the dorms to start her freshman year. She had a first-floor room, a roommate, a lofted bed with a desk underneath, the whole college dorm experience. One morning, when her roommate was sleeping over at her boyfriend's apartment, Sara woke up with a man on top of her. This was not a drunken hook-up, this was a stranger. A man who had somehow managed to climb through Sara's window and up the ladder onto her platform bed without being detected.

Sara's nightmare scenario isn't a common one. Twenty-eight percent of sexual assaults are perpetrated by strangers,[*] but the reality is, women like Sara are much more likely to be attacked by someone they know. That statistical unlikelihood didn't make Sara's situation any less real. She could smell this strange man. He was grabbing at her. By the time Sara could clear the cobwebs from her brain, he had her pinned and was about to pull back the sheets. Most young women's first reaction in this scenario would be to scream. Not Sara. She instantly recognized the situation she was in. Her first reaction wasn't a reaction at all, it was a thought: "He's not close enough."

During our training aboard the cruise ship, we ran the girls through a series of sexual assault scenarios. One of the things we taught them was that after a man grabs you, in order to perpetrate a rape he will have to move in at least two ways: 1) he will have to remove, unzip, or pull down his pants, and 2) he will have to remove or pull down any of her clothing obstructing his path. In this scenario, he would also have to pull down the comforter and sheets under which Sara was sleeping. When that moment of adjustment occurs, the attacker will have to loosen control of her body and remove at least one of his hands from her. Doing so would also bring him closer to her and expose one of his most vulnerable body parts—his face.

So, Sara waited. The next thing she realized was that to escape this situation unharmed she would have to inflict an

---

[*] According to the Rape, Abuse & Incest National Network (RAINN) and a 2015 Department of Justice survey on national crime victimization. https://www.rainn.org/statistics/perpetrators-sexual-violence

injury (we will cover the concept of injury in great depth in Chapter Six). She wasn't going to escape by yelling—only by *doing*, and by doing something *terrible*. Pinned to her back, with his legs positioned inside hers, the only vulnerable body part she could reach was the man's eyes. (It was one of several body parts we trained briefly with her cruise group.)

Sure enough, the man began to adjust. He pulled down the sheets and then his pants, forcing him to lean in closer to her. That's when Sara snapped into action. She wrapped her left arm around the back of his neck, and attacked his left eye with her right hand. She remembered from the seminar that when you attack anywhere on an assailant's face—but especially the eyes—they are going to move away from you violently. This is both an instinctive self-preservation response and an attempt to retain control of the situation by pulling away from the attack. If you're a young woman like Sara, who weighed probably 110 pounds at the time, that means you can't let up. You don't have the same margin of error as a man or a larger woman. You literally have to hang on for dear life, and keep attacking. (Remember what happened to Diane when she scratched blindly at her attacker's face?)

Sara's attacker was easily 235 pounds, and strong. When she dug into his eye, he wrenched back in the opposite direction like a rodeo bull. Their combined momentum pulled them both off the lofted bed and onto the hardwood floor below. Knowing something like this was going to happen, Sara focused on her grip around the back of the man's neck and latched on. While her grip around his neck stayed secure as they fell to the floor, she lost her grip on his eye and her forearm slipped down his face. This was not a conscious decision on Sara's part, but as they hit the ground, she sent all her 110 gravity-aided pounds through her right forearm and into his throat.

She felt the injury happen right as they hit the ground. His body went weak. Any vile intention his brain may have been conjuring became moot the moment his body ceased to function at its command. This gave Sara the opportunity she needed to get away and run screaming down the hall for help. By the time campus security got to her room, the man had asphyxiated and died right where they'd landed.*

Can you imagine yourself in Sara's situation? Someone bigger, faster, and stronger than you, crawling silently into your bed? Can you imagine having the guts to stay calm and plan your attack? Sara had guts. She had composure. And the thing that anchored both of those traits was her *training*. The second the man grabbed her, Sara told me it was like I was in her ear. This is a foundational truth about violence and self-protection: When random violence finds you, you're only ever going to be able to do what you've trained to do, and you're only going to be able to draw from your established knowledge base. Sara had just one training session (which she didn't even want to be in), and from that limited exposure to instruction alone she knew three important things: that she couldn't compete with her attacker's size,

---

* When campus and local police investigated the events, they discovered that the man was a serial rapist who had been terrorizing that campus and a couple others in the area for nearly six years. He had been watching her for three weeks. He knew her roommate spent every other night at her boyfriend's place. He tested their first-floor window and found they often left it unlocked. Investigators found his notes among his possessions.

that she would need to inflict an injury, and that once she did, she had to stay on it. All this information was stored in her brain for instant recall when her life was at stake. (See Chapter Seven for our discussion of the brain as your deadliest weapon.)

HESITATION KILLS

In 1997, on a busy country highway in Carthage, Texas, a twenty-three-year-old police officer named Michelle Jeter pulled over a beat-up blue minivan for speeding. Officer Jeter began the routine traffic stop by the book, asking the driver for his license and ordering him to step out of the vehicle. The driver was a thirty-seven-year-old man named Jorge Orozco. He had his eight-year-old daughter with him, who stayed in the front passenger seat, as he exited the minivan and joined Officer Jeter on the shoulder of the road. Jeter then moved to her patrol car and radioed in Orozco's driver's license number with a request to search for warrants and criminal history.

While waiting for the background check results, Officer Jeter made conversation with Orozco and casually asked him if he'd ever been to jail before. He had. When the check came back it revealed multiple outstanding traffic warrants from the Texas Department of Public Safety. At this point, Officer Jeter asked Orozco for permission to search the vehicle. He consented and his daughter joined him on the side of the road. At first glance, the van was full of furniture and other personal belongings, but since there was not a clear view into the back, Officer Jeter had to open things up and look deeper inside. When she discovered a duffel bag containing marijuana, she went into detainment mode. She turned from the van's driver-side door and corralled Orozco from the back of the van toward the hood of her patrol car, on which she ordered him to place his hands while she readied her handcuffs with one hand, and radioed for backup with the other.

We know all this because the events were captured by the dashboard camera in Officer Jeter's patrol car. The dash cam also shows that while Jeter was searching the vehicle, Orozco had started to get agitated. He was pacing nervously, muttering to himself. Even without the benefit of knowing how this story ends, you get the sense that this guy probably wasn't going to go quietly.

As Officer Jeter moved Orozco toward the car he asked her repeatedly, "What's wrong?", rocking oddly back and forth from one leg to the other, almost like a boxer. She got him to the car and he put his right hand down on the hood. She was directly behind him at that point. For a second it looked like everything was going to go according to procedure. But the next second, instead of putting his left hand on the car next to his right, Orozco turned around. Orozco, 5'10" and 220 pounds, was now face to face with Jeter, 5'5" and 125 pounds. This was the moment—the moment he was going to decide whether to give up or run. But all Officer Jeter could see was the little girl.

The two-year Carthage PD veteran with an exemplary service record thought to herself, *there's no way a man would do anything in front of his child that would traumatize her.* She asked herself, *if I were getting arrested in front of my little girl, how would I want the police officer to act toward me?* In seconds, Jeter had fabricated in her mind a kind of social contract with Orozco in which he wouldn't act violently and she wouldn't initiate violence, either.

Proper procedure in this situation is very clear: the instant Orozco turned to face Jeter, she should have increased the distance and escalated through the force continuum—beginning with firm verbal commands, then moving to pepper spray, the baton, and her firearm as necessary—like she was trained by her department. Instead, Jeter hesitated. Not because the moment was too big for her. Not because it moved too fast. Not for too long either. Just the second and a half it took Orozco to make his fateful decision. While her empathy for Orozco's daughter kept her hand away from the tools on her utility belt a split second longer that it should have, Orozco planted his right hand squarely into Officer Jeter's jaw. He knocked her to the ground, straddled her body, and pummeled her into uncon-sciousness. Right in front of his eight-year-old daughter. The entire violent encounter lasted nine seconds. Jeter's hesi-tancy to use violence and Orozco's willingness to engage it immediately put them on a crash course that resulted in one of the most vicious officer assaults ever captured on video.*

And I want to be very clear about this: if Jeter, as a police officer, was mistaken to hesitate in that situation, you, as a private citizen, would be even more mistaken to hesitate in a similar situation. Officer Jeter was sworn to serve and

---

* Officer Jeter spent six days in a medically induced coma and underwent lengthy facial reconstruction to repair her left eye, left cheek, nose, and part of her jaw. Orozco was eventually arrested and sentenced to sixty years in prison.

protect, and she had a mandate that extended beyond self-protection—for instance, de-escalating an encounter that involved an innocent child as a bystander. It's tragic that her attempt to balance those responsibilities with self-protection put her life in such severe danger. But that's why we honor law enforcement officers for doing their jobs—because they take on *more* responsibilities than the rest of us. As a private citizen in a similar situation, your case is like Officer Jeter's in one key way: in both, hesitation kills. But because your mandate is *less* complicated than hers—protect your own life, period—you have even less excuse for hesitation.

In either case, hesitation—the difference between acting and reacting—can be the difference between life and death. In all my studies of self-protection, training and debriefing military units and law enforcement agencies, examining security footage from prison yards and talking to prison guards, I have discovered that the odds of winning a violent encounter swing precipitously in favor of whoever inflicts the first debilitating injury. That doesn't mean anytime you feel nervous or fearful that you should impulsively look for stray chef's knives or ready yourself for well-timed eye gouges. You should always endeavor to remove yourself from any situation in which you are uncomfortable. What it *does* mean, however, is that if you are getting asocial cues from someone, you need to act. If violence becomes inevitable and inescapable, you must *never* hesitate to harness your knowledge and lean on your training to protect yourself. You must never let thoughts about what violence *means* or *says* delay its utilization, because in those moments where it is necessary, there is no room for nuance and semantics. There is no time to parse a predator's intent, to figure out what is going on inside their head, to understand how they think and what kind of moral code they have (or don't have). Even if there were time, those things are basically unknowable.

Your power is in your knowledge and understanding of violence, in your awareness and preparedness, in your training and capacity to act. Every time you shrink from an act of violence like those Diane and Sara endured, or you project empathy toward a person who is showing you their true colors, or you choose to make some directionless prayer like, "I hope that never happens to me!", you are relinquishing all that power. You are giving first-mover advantage to your potentially mortal opponent.

If you take one thing from what you've read so far, I hope it's this: anytime you attempt to bury your head in the sand and deny the existence of violence in *your* world, not only are you giving up your power, but you are giving it over to the very perpetrators of random violence whose existence you are hoping to ignore.

Instead, look violence in the eyes and ask yourself, "How did that work?" Because in learning what the tool of violence truly is and how it really works, we remind ourselves that the perpetrators of violence are human beings—the same as us. We possess the same abilities, with access to the same tools. The difference between us is not in the "what," but in the "why."

CHAPTER TWO

SOCIAL AGGRESSION VERSUS ASOCIAL VIOLENCE

Dulce bellum inexpertis. (War is sweet to those who have never experienced it.)

—*Pindar*

You don't have to look very hard on YouTube to find videos of long-suffering kids reaching their breaking point with bullies and finally fighting back. The scenes vary in geography, gender, and the size and age difference of the kids involved, but each scene generally goes down the same way.

The video picks up mid-conflict. The bully is in full aggressor mode: stalking after the victim, cutting them off, pushing them, taunting them, and getting in their envelope of personal space, sometimes looming over them like a beast. The bullying victim is folded over, trying to make themselves smaller. Or they're turned to the side, as if subconsciously hoping the teasing will just go away. Sometimes they're backed against a wall, as if they are hoping to melt into it.

Then, suddenly, there is a shift. The victim stops, stiffens, and bows up. There is going to be a fight. The bully is almost always caught off-guard when this happens. Bullies typically pick their victims based on the likelihood that they won't fight back. The fight might happen right then and there, it might have to wait until after school. It doesn't really matter, though, because once the bully's victim has had enough and finally decides to defend himself, the decision ripples through the playground or the schoolyard like a shockwave. The other kids start getting super excited. If the fight is going down after school, it's all anyone can talk about. *They can't wait.* If it happens right there in the moment, the kids immediately encircle the pair chanting, "Fight! Fight! Fight!" In the lead-up to the actual physical confrontation, the bully will often start talking trash in an attempt to humiliate or intimidate and regain the upper hand in his relationship to the victim. If the victim responds, it's to show that the bully's taunts aren't going to work this time. They're going to have it out once and for all.

Fights likes these are instances of what I call "social aggression." They are quasi-violent scenarios that stem from conflict and jockeying within the social hierarchy. I call them quasi-violent not because I don't take them seriously, but rather because they don't always involve violence as we understand it—sometimes it's just talking or threatening—and they're less about physically destroying the other person than they are about asserting social dominance, gaining some advantage, or elevating social status. That's why people instinctively *want* to gather around and watch these types of conflicts, because they want to see what happens.

Kids get so excited about these playground fights because there is valuable social information to be gleaned from them. Both fighters' positions in the school's social hierarchy are in flux. The bully occupies a position of power, and when his target finally fights back, that means his position is being challenged. When it's all over, will there be a change in social standing? Will the bully get his comeuppance and be reduced to a pariah and a laughingstock? Will his victim be elevated to the position of nerd hero or defender of the meek and helpless? Or will the bully get the upper hand and the social status remain the same? This kind of aggression isn't exactly tolerated—it's the kind teachers usually break up and punish, after all—but it doesn't destroy the social order in the school, either. Afterward, the kids will be talking about it excitedly in the lunchroom for the rest of the week.

And then there is the other way these playground fights and bully takedowns can go. These are the kinds of incidents that do not show up on YouTube. The victim has had enough, but he has only stiffened and bowed up in his mind. He—and it's almost always a he—has no interest in fighting back at the center of a ring of classmates. Instead, he opens his backpack, pulls out a revolver, and shoots his bully in the head at point blank range. Do you want to guess what happens next? There is no excited chanting for a fight. No one is hoisting the bully's victim on their shoulders and marching him triumphantly around the schoolyard. There is only complete and total pandemonium. Everybody runs and no one looks back. There is no social information to be gathered here.

That is the rough outline of any number of the school and workplace shootings that have dominated our news over the past fifteen years, and become (along with ISIS-style terrorism) the scariest, most urgent form of violence we face today. I call violence of this nature "asocial." Asocial violence is violence that has nothing to do with communication or reshuffling the pecking order. Asocial violence is nothing like that: it doesn't try to change the order, it tries to *wreck* the order. It's the kind of violent interaction we instinctively run from—the kind in which there is only mayhem, death, misery, and horror. (The knockout game is asocial violence.) At the end of the day, all violence has the potential to be a matter of life or death. The difference with asocial violence is that death and destruction are not its by-products; they are its purpose.

It is essential we understand this distinction between social aggression and asocial violence right now. Social aggression is about competition; asocial violence is about destruction. Competition has rules; destruction has none. Social aggression is about communication—implicitly with status indicators but explicitly with lots of taunting and posturing. There is no talking with asocial violence. Open your mouth and you are likely to eat a lightning-fast punch or a jacketed bullet travelling at 2,500 feet per second.

LET'S TALK

If there is one reliable way to distinguish between the two kinds of violent encounter, it is the presence or absence of communication. If a man comes upon you from behind as you're walking home from dinner and he puts a gun to your head and says, "Give me your wallet or I'll blow your brains out," that is fundamentally an act of social aggression. It may *feel* asocial, because you feel powerless when you're taken by surprise, but how you feel has nothing to do with whether a situation is social or asocial. What matters is the intent and the action of the attacker. In this scenario, his primary motive is not to destroy, it's to dominate. He's using the *threat of violence* to make it easier to get what he wants. If the situation were asocial, if what he wanted to do was destroy you, you would not hear any words. You probably wouldn't even hear the hammer cock before the trigger got pulled and the bullet left the chamber.

Social aggression doesn't wear off after adolescence; fast-forward twelve years to a bar fight between rival fraternity members and the outline is the same. It's still two guys exhibiting their inner-male aggression, thrashing, ranting, raving. It's the silverback gorilla banging his chest. It's the butting of rams' heads. It's the clashing of male grizzly bears. These are all bids for a kind of social status, and they're all meant to be witnessed.

The schoolyard brawl and the bar fight aren't usually life-or-death situations. Rather, they're a form of primitive communication. It's a social display that communicates, *"I'm really agitated. I'm mad. I want to run this other guy off my territory."* And the other guy is responding, *"I'm not willing to be run off my territory. I'm going to stand my ground."* The intent is not to inflict grievous bodily harm. It's only to exert social dominance.

In these situations of quasi-violence, people rarely punch their opponent's throat or kick them in the testicles or gouge out their eyes. They rarely try to inflict permanent damage. If you were to look at such a confrontation simply from the perspective of causing bodily harm, you'd call it wildly inefficient. I have studied video of countless epic bar brawls that have gone on for ten or fifteen minutes that left the combatants bloody and bruised, but also conscious, uninjured, and able to walk away. I've also seen guys beat each other senseless and then hang out afterward—like it was something they just needed to get out of their systems.

Many of us know how to act like jerks and add fuel to the fire, how to turn an argument into a shouting match that turns into a fistfight. It can be scary. It can be wrong. It can be extremely intimidating. But the aggressor is not deliberately trying to maim, cripple, or kill. He's not trying to break down the social order, to sow terror and mistrust. The goal is to dominate, not to destroy. This is social aggression.

Asocial violence, on the other hand, is brutally streamlined. It's quiet. It happens suddenly and unmistakably. It's one person beating another person with a tire iron until he stops moving. It's stabbing somebody thirty-seven times. It's pulling a gun and firing round after round until he goes down, and then stepping close to make sure he has two to the brain, just to be sure. If you're a sane, socialized person, thoughts like those can make you physically ill. That's because you recognize them for what they are: the breakdown of everything we, as humans, hold sacred. Indeed, they are often a breakdown of the perpetrator of the violence themselves. They are no longer in control, they are no longer thinking rationally, they are no longer thinking at all. These acts represent the destruction of the social fabric. They're devoid of honor. They're acts without rules, where anything goes.

So why am I harping on the difference? Because our responses to social aggression and asocial violence ought to be fundamentally different.

Social aggression is avoidable—and you *should* avoid it. You can choose not to participate. You can employ social skills to remove yourself from the situation, or to de-escalate it. It comes with big, flashing warning signs—loud, dramatic, and recognizable social posturing. You can see it coming a mile away. These sorts of problems can usually be handled with social tools that we all know how to use. We've all talked our way out of a bad situation. We all know how to calm another person down. We all know how to back down ourselves. If we didn't, none of us would have made it this far in life. Similarly, threats of violence with a clear purpose—like a robbery— can be terrifying. But they remain social interactions, with generally clear demands and big, flashing warning signs of their own; the lines of communication remain open. When he says, "Give me your wallet or I'll blow your brains out," give him your wallet and live to see another day.

You can rarely, if ever, talk yourself out of asocial violence. You have no idea whether the movie theater you chose is the one where a shooter with a full arsenal will show up looking like The Joker and acting like Bane.* You have no idea if your child's school is the one where a deranged mind will decide to make his mark. Asocial violence doesn't care about your social skills. Negotiating with a serial killer is like arguing with a bullet. If it's coming your way, words won't deflect it. If somebody has decided to stab you to death, capitulation doesn't appease them. It only makes their work easier. When it comes to asocial violence, if you have not been able to foresee and escape it, you must render your attacker one of three ways to survive: incapacitated, unconscious, or dead. Understanding and accepting that reality, then training to deal with

---

* Which is what James Holmes did, killing twelve and injuring seventy during a showing of "The Dark Knight Rises" in the 2012 Aurora theater massacre.

these unlikely scenarios, will give you the confidence you need to quickly and calmly identify the difference between social aggression and asocial violence, while setting your mind at ease that you'll be able to handle whichever comes your way—de-escalating where it's possible to de-escalate, and fighting to save your life where it is not.

ANGRY, AGGRESSIVE, DEADLY?

Verbal communication aside, distinguishing between social aggression and asocial violence in the moment is all about looking at the fighting posture of the aggressor. Once they have crossed the physical plane, as I call it, you can tell how serious someone is about inflicting harm by where he places himself to get the job done and how he uses his body to do it.

In social aggression scenarios, angry fighters will step up within striking distance of their opponent but not so close— maybe a half-step away—that they can't dodge a wild punch. Stepping up to your opponent and reaching out is the hall-mark of social aggression: cuffing, shoving, and punching to show displeasure. It shows a lack of desire to cripple and kill, it signals a healthy fear of the other man, and even a bit of respect for his personal space—it is, after all, giving him plenty of room to work. It says, "I'm pissed off, but there are still rules here." As a result, injury is relatively unlikely in these kinds of confrontations, outside of a freak traumatic brain injury—which is the most common fight-ending injury we see in both street fights and competitive matches. (Usually they're stopped well before that point by friends, teachers, referees, etc.)

Fights in the stands at a sporting event are a good example of this kind of confrontation: lots of shoving, flailing punches, glancing blows that stun but don't injure. Even more illustrative are schoolyard fights between teenage girls. There is lots of pushing to maintain distance, windmill punching, and hair-pulling. Once both fighters have a firm grip on the other's hair, the fight often deadlocks with each girl bent over at the waist ninety degrees, or sprawled flat on the ground, their arms fully locked out an impossible distance away from each other so that neither can land a punch. They look like deer with their antlers interlocked (which itself is a social competition display, coincidentally).

Some fighters, though, go from angry to aggressive and will gladly go toe-to-toe with you. Their trash talk gets inside your head as their bodies get inside your personal space, underneath your center of gravity. This is an escalation of posture that brings intimidation into play, but also increased effectiveness: the proximity will allow for greater follow-through, dramatically increasing the chance of injury and knockdown. These guys will push each other and go head-hunting, looking to punch each other in the face to shut off communication. They get aggressive because they literally want to shut you up, which is a hallmark of drunken bar fights and street fights. They are still in the realm of social aggression.

Then there are killers. The killer does not intimidate or talk trash. The killer doesn't talk, period. Nor does he step up to his opponent or inside their personal space. He steps *through* his opponent. He doesn't punch, he penetrates. He sends his entire body through his belt buckle, across the physical plane, and through the other man until he stands where the other man once stood. This maximizes injury and overrun, almost guaranteeing that his blows will knock his enemy down. And when the enemy is down, he doesn't stop. He wants to erase and replace him. He goes to the ground with him, and doesn't stop until his enemy is utterly disabled. This is not the kind of fight you stick around to watch. There is no rooting interest here, no social information to be gleaned.

That is the knockout game at its worst. That is the school or workplace shooting. That is Jorge Orozco and Officer Jeter. When Orozco turned on the 5'5" Jeter, he didn't push her away or swing wildly to create some distance so he could run. He didn't get up in the smaller woman's face to intimidate her. He instantly closed the distance and put himself right through her, driving her into the ground with nine closed-fist blows to the face in nine seconds that nearly killed her.

That is asocial violence.

WHEN THE RULES DON'T APPLY

Though these kinds of conflict—social aggression and asocial violence—look and sound quite different from each other, our instinct is to apply the same set of rules to both, because our socialized minds don't want to accept the possibility that the rare and unthinkable has found us, by no fault of our own. If we don't have rules governing how we deal with the rare and unthinkable, then the rare and unthinkable can't happen, right? Alternatively, we try to shove this unseemly business out of our minds by dismissing the distinction altogether: *Why are we talking about this? Violence is violence; it's all bad*. We get ourselves into deep trouble when we take either one of these approaches, because you can't play by rules that your attacker refuses to recognize even exist.

Rules, as a social construct, only work in a conflict when both sides honor them. Major League Baseball has a broad set of rules that generalize across the American and National Leagues. But when teams from each league play against each other during interleague play or in the World Series, they have to agree on which league's rules govern or else the whole thing collapses. The idea that rules of any kind go away the second *the other guy* ignores them is generally unsettling and downright terrifying in the case of violence. But when you think about asocial violence through that prism, you start to realize that it's a horrible mistake to use the same social contract that governs social aggression, to understand and navigate true asocial violence. During true violence, our usual social categories—good guy/bad guy, right/wrong, attacker/defender—cease to apply. These dichotomies are useful, but only before and after a violent confrontation has occurred. During the actual fight, they are utterly irrelevant, if not misleading and dangerous.

For instance, before the action, the idea of "self-defense" is defined morally. The moral right to defend oneself from an attack is what puts violently attempting a rape and violently fighting off a rapist on opposing sides of the moral spectrum. No one would put Sara in the "bad guy" category for striking back at her rapist and accidentally killing him in the process.

After the action, "self-defense" becomes a legal question: it's civil society deciding whether to give you an official pass for using violence to protect yourself or save your life. No jury would rule that what Sara did was "illegal."

But *during* the action, those questions go out the window. It is an issue of practicality in the most literal sense. In the midst of a violent encounter, to think merely of "defending" yourself—rather than incapacitating your opponent—is essentially to curl up in a ball and hope for the best. Waiting for your attacker to give up—or worse, expecting him to *follow the rules*—is, putting it bluntly, to risk participating in your own murder. Your only reliable course of action to save your life is to do what your attacker is trying to do to you, but do it more effectively and efficiently, and to do it first. To use the very same tool of violence.

And yet, as sane, socialized beings, we continue to drag our rules into these places where they don't belong. We want to somehow keep everything fair, on a level playing field. This is why most confrontations involving real violence go terribly wrong for the good guy. We're constrained by a litany of social rules while the asocial predator is bound only by the laws of physics. All he cares about is how best and most quickly he can do you grievous bodily harm and end the situation. He'll stab you when you're not looking. He'll kick you in the throat when you're down. If things don't look hot for him, he'll capitulate to get you to let go, then pull his gun and shoot you. He'll use your socialization against you— he'll turn the social rules that normally protect you from harm into his most powerful weapon. But all his weapons are tools that you can use in turn.

When you're staring down the barrel of a gun (literally and figuratively) with a violent asocial predator on the other end of it, you must remember that this is not a movie or a video game or a hero fantasy. This is not high noon at the O.K. Corral. There is no Good, Bad, and Ugly—there is just ugly.

THINGS CAN TURN ON A DIME

In 2006, a young British lawyer named Thomas Pryce exited the tube station by his home. It was early January, about eleven-thirty at night. It was cold. Tom had just left a work function in London and he was hustling back to the flat he shared with his fiancée on a quiet street in an up-and-coming suburb of London.

On this night, he was followed by two young men in hooded sweatshirts who had robbed someone else earlier in the evening and saw Tom as another opportunity. They circled around in front of him and drew their knives, demanding his valuables. He quickly complied, handing over everything. If the incident had ended there, we might say that Tom used his social skills to escape an instance of social aggression. He saw assailants who, however intimidating and dangerous, were still offering a recognizable, if coercive, exchange—his possessions for his life, straight up—and he accepted the exchange. He kept quiet, offered no resistance, and gave up his property exactly how the authorities tell you to do it in a robbery situation like that.

Thomas was shaken up, but he kept walking home. Then the young men came back. This time, their knives were already drawn, their heads were down, and they weren't saying anything. Thomas broke into a sprint, but they quickly overtook him and began stabbing him repeatedly, in the chest, the hip, the face, the hands, and the lower torso. He yelled frantically, "Why, why, why? You've got everything!" But they didn't have everything. They didn't have the one thing they needed once they realized he had seen their faces. They didn't have his silence.

"He could identify us," they said to themselves, according to the Metropolitan police who interrogated the men upon their capture, *"we need to kill him."* That quick realization was all it took for those two young men to go from opportunistic robbers to cold-blooded murderers. Social aggression to asocial violence in the blink of an eye.

The lesson I take from Tom's murder is how essential it is to understand the difference between the two types of physical confrontation. You need to be able to identify them in the moment, and you need to recognize that one can turn into the other very quickly when circumstances change. The kind of encounter that Tom endured initially—no matter how frightening it must have been—still presumed a kind of communication. He was in the kind of conflict that we can escape with our social skills: after all, giving up your belongings in exchange for your life is a kind of negotiation, even if it happens under extreme duress. If you can comply with demands, it means there's still communication happening, which means there's still a chance of getting out of there in one piece.

Unfortunately, the situation turned asocial very quickly, for reasons Tom could not have foreseen. The rules that he believed were governing his initial encounter ceased to apply when the two men returned. His attempts to communicate, to negotiate, to make sense of what was happening, all of it fell on deaf ears and was met only with more violence. His only hope lay in recognizing, quickly, what kind of situation he was in, and acting accordingly. In a phrase: *using violence.* By the time he realized the shift from social aggression to asocial violence — if he ever realized it — it was too late.

To be fair to Tom, his was not an unreasonable or uncommon response. We've seen it many times before. In one infamous incident from 1994, the husband of figure skater Tonya Harding hired a man named Shane Stant to break the leg of Tonya's main rival, Nancy Kerrigan, so that she would be unable to compete at the 1994 Winter Olympics in Lillehammer, Norway.

Stant made his move after an early January practice session in Detroit just as Kerrigan came off the ice, smashing her a few inches above the knee of her right leg with a telescopic police baton. Stant failed to break Kerrigan's leg — only badly bruising it — but the footage captured immediately after the incident shows an understandably hysterical Kerrigan on the ground holding her leg, repeatedly shouting "Why, why, why?" Unlike Thomas, she wasn't trying to reason with her attacker, but she was trying to reason with the universe. The rules by which her world operated don't account for this kind of violence. Something important to keep in mind is that just because this happened in the context of personal rivalry and competition, doesn't mean it wasn't also asocial. The Harding camp was not trying to intimidate or dominate Kerrigan; it was trying to destroy her.

Stant blindsided and cold-cocked Kerrigan. There was absolutely nothing she could have done differently to protect herself. But Tom Pryce's situation was a little different. When escape was off the table, the only thing that could have helped him was a fuller understanding of the tool of violence and greater preparedness to take immediate action. Instead of turning to flee, he needed to turn and fight. Because when an aggressor doesn't care about your reasons or your rules, and isn't interested in having a negotiation, no other strategy tends to work. Especially when you're outnumbered. Tom's only hope was to inflict injury first. But before his survival depended on that, it depended on recognizing, as soon as possible, that he was not in a situation of coercion and communication, but in a situation of life-or-death violence.*

THE SCARIEST GUY IN THE ROOM

For any semi-self-aware individual, it's clear quickly that two hooded men following you home in the middle of the night are probably not good dudes. That's an easy determination to make when it's you, two strangers, and an empty street. But what about at a bar or a music festival or a state fair?

Let me spare you the suspense: the scariest guy in the room is rarely the tattooed weightlifter making snarling faces and threatening gestures. That guy, while potentially dangerous, is openly and obviously posturing to stake his position in the immediate social hierarchy. The guy you need to worry about is the one you don't suspect. The one who doesn't posture or talk. The one who, if he really wanted to harm you, would quietly slide the blade out of his pocket without drawing attention to himself and get it done.

In the mid-1980s, San Diego was a pretty rough place. The post-college crowd hadn't found the city yet and we were

---

* "Man blames his friend for murder," BBC News, November 16, 2006, news.bbc.co.uk/2/hi/uk_news/england/london/6154234.stm.

still a couple decades away from the influx of people from other California cities getting priced out of their areas and coming down for the cheaper cost of living. Back then it was still mostly a military town and a way station between Mexico and all points north and east. It could get pretty hairy.

After getting medically rolled from the SEALs after my inner-ear injury, I had some time to figure out what my next move was going to be. I spent a fair amount of that at a notoriously tough bar called Jose Murphy's, where my brother worked as a bouncer. This was one of those bars where all the local cops knew all the bouncers by first name, and vice versa. Members of the Hells Angels and Mongols motorcycle clubs were frequent visitors. Fights were a nightly attraction.

The lead bouncer at Jose Murphy's around this time was a guy named Mike. Mike was 6'8", fully tattooed, and built like a dump truck. Nobody messed with Mike and, understanding his obvious size advantage and natural intimidation factor, he didn't mess with anyone unless he absolutely had to. One weekend was especially rough. The place was totally packed. There were fights every other hour, it seemed, for two or three days straight. There was never any downtime for Mike to relax and catch his breath. He had the perfect temperament for a bouncer, but even he had his limitations.

Last call on the final night of the weekend could not come soon enough. When it finally arrived, Mike turned on the lights, cut the music, and started ushering customers out the door. People who got in under the wire for a last round were encouraged to drink up and get out. Wisely, most people complied. But there was this one guy at the end of the bar who just wouldn't budge. He was unremarkable and skinny, hunched quietly, sipping away at his beer, ignoring the orders to leave. He hadn't made trouble the whole night, keeping entirely to himself. That didn't earn him any brownie points with Mike at two a.m., however. Mike wanted to get the hell out of there, go home, and wash off the last couple days.

Like any good bouncer, Mike gave the guy three chances. The first one was a heads-up to all the customers that the bar was closing. The second one was a direct warning to the guy at the end of the bar. The third one involved taking his drink and physically removing him off the barstool. When even that didn't work, Mike's frustration boiled over and he got aggressive. He got in the guy's face, towering over him, collapsing every centimeter of personal space, then trying to move him off his stool, and finally dropping him to the ground. It was a classic instance of social aggression. Mike wasn't trying to inflict injury—he was asserting his position as the bouncer and showing his dominance over this patch of real estate. Unfortunately, the other guy didn't read it that way.

What Mike hadn't noticed while he loomed over the uncooperative patron was the blade he'd quietly slipped out of his boot. He wasn't on the ground for more than two seconds, but in that time he managed to slit Mike's left Achilles tendon and, on the way up to his feet, slash his femoral artery. He immediately slid out the back door, and before anyone knew what was happening, Mike was in a heap on the ground in the middle of a quickly expanding pool of blood.

Mike was having a bad day, he was exhausted at the end of a long shift, he got sloppy, and he let this guy, who wasn't the last one to leave and wasn't overtly being a jerk, get under his skin. Mike also had the great misfortune of getting over-confident with his size and his social position. He misread the man across from him, thinking by size disparity alone that he couldn't possibly pose a threat. But the man turned out to be a convicted felon and career criminal who came from a world where the kind of imminent threat that Mike was posing was almost always a lethal, asocial one and should be responded to swiftly and in kind.*

The good news is that true criminal sociopaths like this are rare, just as asocial violence is rare compared to social aggression. The bad news is there's no way to identify them, just as there is no way to read their minds or guess their intent.

I tried to teach my son Conner that lesson the summer before he went off to college. I arranged through some law enforcement buddies to take him on a tour of the Clark County Detention Center (CCDC) in Las Vegas. The CCDC is a medium-security facility in downtown Las Vegas that can house up to one thousand inmates—many of them violent offenders. As the guards got everything set for our tour, Conner and I sat in the processing area and watched as the staff brought in new inmates just starting their sentences, and released others who'd just finished theirs.

Our first stop was the cafeteria, where inmates were fed three times a day, hundreds at a time. Like a typical young kid who was nervous and unsure, Conner approached the entrance to the cafeteria with his hands in his sweatshirt pockets. The guard spotted it right away.

"Hey! Get your hands out of your pockets."

It startled Conner for a second, so the guard explained.

---

* Thankfully, we were able to stop the bleeding from Mike's leg and get him to a hospital in time to save his life.

"Those guys in there are on constant lookout for threats. Danger can come from anywhere and anyone at any time. They've never seen you before, they have no idea who you are. And you come in there with your hands in your pockets? That's a double red flag."

Sure enough, we walk into the cafeteria and it's like a record scratch. Everyone stops what they're doing and immediately sizes us both up: Threat or not a threat? It was probably the first time Conner was conscious of another human being looking at him and figuring out if he might have to kill him at some point.

The rest of the tour was uneventful but enlightening. When we walked out the front door of the CCDC, Conner reoriented himself and made for the car. I stopped him and told him to come back over by me and look two blocks down the street.

"What do you see down there?" I asked him.

"That's Fremont Street."

"What's in there?"

"Shops."

"What else?"

"Tourists."

"How many tourists do you think are down there right now?"

"I don't know, a thousand maybe?"

"Remember all those guys we watched walk out of this prison when we were waiting to start the tour?"

"Uh-huh."

"You think any of them maybe went down there?"

"Maybe, yeah."

"Okay, go find them."

"What do you mean?"

"Go in there and see if you can find them."

"That's impossible."

"Exactly."

Some of those men who sized up Conner in the CCDC were garden-variety thieves and drug dealers. Perhaps a handful were violent sociopaths. But there was no telling them apart on sight in the cafeteria, just as there was no telling any of those criminals apart on sight from the ordinary people on Fremont Street. That was my lesson for Conner: you can't tell just by sight who's a good guy and who's a bad guy. Each one of the men who walked out of CCDC that day was, the day before, one of the guys in the cafeteria who stopped cold to size us up as potential threats. And if my experience watching Mike nearly bleed out twenty-five years earlier at the hands of a man half his size was any indication, there was no telling which one of those newly free men was the scariest, either.

But remember: all of what I've been explaining goes both ways. Just as there's no way to de-escalate a situation of true, asocial violence, there's no reason to escalate a situation of social aggression. We learn the difference between the two not only to prepare ourselves to fight for our lives when we absolutely have to, but also to prepare ourselves to wisely back down when there's no need for a fight.

CHAPTER THREE

MINDSET MATTERS MOST

Engage your mind before you engage your weapon... the most important six inches on the battlefield are between your ears.

> —*United States Secretary of Defense,*
> *General James N. Mattis (USMC, Ret.)*

Look at this image. Imagine this is you. Imagine that the unthinkable has happened and random asocial violence has found you. What would you do? Really think about it. What's your first move?

While you're thinking, let me tell you what *I* would do.

My first move would be to continue choking my attacker. As his focus moves to getting my hands off him, it will expose his midsection and I will drive my knee into his groin. Bent over now, with his head leaning forward, his center of gravity will be out past his knees, which will allow me to grab his head and slam it down into the ground. And then reach down and slam it again. If he's not completely incapacitated at this point and still poses a threat, I will step over him and drop my knee on his throat.

You were expecting me to think of myself as the figure on the right, weren't you? If you're anything like the overwhelming majority of people who attend my seminars, you answer that way because seeing ourselves any other way is unthinkable. Even now, three chapters into this book, the mental image I just sketched for you has you pressed back against your seat as you subconsciously try to distance yourself from the brutality. I want you to be honest with yourself. Where did you see yourself? The one being choked, or the one doing the choking? That self-reflection is important.

In February, 2015, I gave a talk called "The Paradox of Violence" at a TEDx event in Grand Forks, North Dakota. I joined a remarkable group of authors, educators, entrepreneurs, and experts from a variety of fields who'd trekked up to the frozen tundra of North Dakota in the middle of winter to give their own talks around the theme of "Launch." My goal was to set audience members on a new trajectory for thinking about and understanding violence.

The image I placed at the beginning of this chapter was going to be an important part of my presentation. Unfortunately, not being the biggest event in the world, the TEDx-GrandForks organizers had not secured a projector for my use. So instead, near the end of my eighteen-minute talk, I brought two young men up onstage with me. It was clear right away that the guys who volunteered as my living models were uncomfortable with the role play that was about to take place.

I spent about thirty seconds setting up the scenario, then had the young men freeze in tableau when they found the same position as the figures in my training image. I gave the audience a few beats to process what they were looking at, then I asked them by a show of hands to tell me which of the two men they identified with. Nearly every person immediately placed themselves in the role of the victim, despite having *just* listened to me talk for seventeen minutes about the importance of not becoming a victim. That's how ingrained this thought pattern has become in our society. Think about that: Culturally, we instinctively see ourselves as the victim.*

Most people look at this simple image and place themselves in the shoes of the person in the compromised position for two reasons: First, our empathy kicks in and, not knowing the context, we instantly feel for the person who appears to be the victim. Second, we cannot imagine ourselves being capable of choking someone, deliberately trying to hurt them. We're not violent people. We've been taught our whole lives to be polite and kind and peaceful, that

---

* Isn't it also interesting to consider that, evolutionarily at least, this cannot possibly be how early man would have seen himself. We wouldn't be here if he had.

violence is never the answer, because *we're the good guys*. So, obviously, we *can't* be the one in the dominant position.

From the perspective of ordinary social life, that is a normal, healthy way to think. Empathy keeps us human and defaulting away from aggression keeps us civilized. But if you're concerned with self-protection, imagining yourself in the shoes of the person being attacked is the worst possible way to think. It is the beginning of your vulnerability to asocial violence. You must remember that violence is a tool, not a moral proposition. Using it effectively when you have no other choice doesn't say anything about whether you're a "good guy" or a "bad guy." But if you tell yourself that it does, then it follows that a "good guy" could never get the upper hand in a fight, which means you've convinced yourself that "good guy" equals "victim." We're so used to equating "good guy" and "victim" that imagining ourselves on the winning end of a real, life-or-death fight seems impossible, almost forbidden. With that attitude, if you ever find yourself in a fight for your life, it's basically over before it has even begun.

CRIMINALS NEVER SEE THEMSELVES AS THE VICTIM

I'll tell you something that should make you shudder: when I show this training image to known criminals—and I have shown it to many of them—they uniformly identify with the figure on the left. They never in a million years imagine themselves as the victim on the receiving end of punishment. They don't hesitate, either. Their response is swift and unequivocal: they're the figure using violence successfully. Sometimes, they even tell me how they'd do the attack better: "You know what he *should* do…"

This gulf in self-perception might be the biggest mental obstacle I have to overcome with my clients—male or female, rich or poor, big or small. It's also the biggest obstacle to keeping yourself safe. It's as if the people who plan to hurt you can speak a language that you've deliberately chosen not to learn. I can (and will in Part 2) teach you all the physical principles of self-protection—punching, kicking, how to throw your body weight and target the vulnerable areas of the human body—but none of that matters if you are not willing to accept that, under the right circumstances, you can be both the "good guy" *and* the guy successfully using violence.

Critical to this shift in perception is the mental preparation necessary for setting your body into action at a moment's notice. This involves hard-wiring yourself with the correct programming in the rare event that an asocial confrontation develops. Specifically, you need to be able to identify what's available to you in terms of weapons and vulnerable body parts, and then you need to be able to inflict injury right away. Taking time to reflect on how you found yourself in this position, or waiting for your assailant to make the first move because you're still thinking about yourself as the good guy on the right, will get you killed.

Predators don't think that way. They don't need to think about what weapons they might grab—they're already wielding one (hint: it's in the six-inch space between their ears). They don't care about what we might do to them during a confrontation. Their only focus is on what they're going to do to *us*. Often this singular obsession is a product of their criminal character, but there is a huge physiological lesson to be learned and strategic advantage to be gained from understanding it. The mind needs clarity to be effective, because it can really only process one thing at a time. The brain's processing power is very fast, but when it counts, a millisecond can be all the difference in the world.

If you are thinking about what your attacker might do, or why he has picked you, then your brain's focus shifts toward the defensive, reactive posture of a victim responding to someone else's aggression, and it puts you way behind the power curve. When you lapse into a defensive mindset like that, you're automatically at a disadvantage, because reacting is *always* slower than acting. While you're thinking, "How will I defend myself if he punches my throat?" your attacker is already punching your throat.

While you're sorting through options, his body has one simple command to follow: hurt them. Kill them. It is this clarity of mind and straightforwardness of action that most often makes the difference between success and failure in actual life-or-death situations. There is no other way around this basic truth: you can't act with the kind of speed and decisiveness necessary to prevail in a violent encounter unless you're mentally prepared to be the guy on the left.

So, spend some time with the training image and think about what you would do if you were in that position, mindful of the fact that there is nothing to learn about violence from its victim, only its perpetrator. Sit with your gut reaction to it, whether it's the "right" one or the "wrong" one. (Say what you will, but you cannot hide your own reaction from yourself.) Think about all the things this training image implies, everything it will require of you to become the one in the driver's seat who is mentally prepared to act when the situation calls for it: from the pressure of your fingers and palms against the Adam's apple and the hyoid bone of the neck, to the feel of a crushed windpipe and collapsed cartilage in the throat, to the sound of asphyxiation once you've gotten the upper hand. These are the lessons of the guy on the left, not the details of a heroic comeback story for the guy on the right.

These are the movements you will need to practice with a partner at a proper training tempo (which we will cover in Chapter Eight), so that if you ever find yourself needing to execute them in real life, it won't be the first time you've choked another human being, but the 301st time. For most people, inflicting debilitating injury like this is such a foreign concept that the kind of deliberate, purposeful visualization I just described feels premeditated, almost pathological. Yet that is precisely the goal, just as it is with every other constructive use of deliberate, purposeful visualization.

Jason Day is one of the most popular professional golfers on the PGA tour, not just for talent or his ability to hit it a long way, but also for his pre-shot routine. It's unlike any other golfer in the game. He addresses the ball, takes two practice swings trying to mimic the feel of the shot he's going to attempt, then he steps behind his ball, closes his eyes and visualizes his shot. It is a very detailed visualization: he has a picture of himself addressing the ball; he has an image of his target, which is small and specific; he sees his swing go back and then come through the ball; he watches the ball take flight; then he follows the trajectory of the ball as it lands and bounces. He does this before every single shot he takes in every single tournament he enters, whether it's on the tee, in the fairway, or on the green, at a pro-am or at the Masters.

The results have been undeniable: He is a major champion, a ten-time winner on the PGA tour, and he's spent extended periods ranked #1 in the world.

Do you know what *never* happens during Jason Day's pre-shot visualization routine? The ball never hooks into the trees. It never goes into the water hazard. He doesn't chunk it into the bunker or fly the green. He doesn't four-putt. No, he stripes it. He hits the ball down the center of the fairway and lands it right where he wants it. His approach shots into the green roll within eight feet of the cup. His putts for birdie, for eagle, *for the win,* land dead center in the middle of the cup with perfect speed.

Why do you suppose that is? Because there's nothing to be gained from imagining failure when we're practicing for victory. And yet that is what we do all the time when it comes to violence. We look at the losing end of a violent encounter—if we allow ourselves to look at anything—and we try to make it work, rather than look at the winning side and try to mimic what worked.

The reason we make this mistake is because we are locked into a mindset where only criminals are successful with violence. Why can only criminals act with such dominance and effective decisiveness? Why can't the good guys win, too? If we continue to tell ourselves that a "good guy" can never get the upper hand in a fight, if we won't even allow ourselves to *imagine* it, then we're setting ourselves up to lose the fight for our lives before it's even begun.

Your goal is the reverse: visualize yourself as the dominant person in the conflict, and remember that you can be dominant and the "good guy" at the same time.

THE FANTASY OF DEFENSE

"What do I do if someone tries to stab me?"

I have had this question posed to me at least a thousand times in my professional career—from students, acquaintances, media, you name it. I know where this conversation will lead, but still I start by offering real, actionable advice they can use to seize the initiative and survive the attack. *Here's how you take his eye, crush his throat, or break his leg.*

Nine times out of ten, the audience member is aghast at the severity of my recommendations. So they rephrase the question.

What they *really* want to know, they say, is "What do I do to prevent someone from stabbing me?" I have answers for that question, too. So do you. We covered some of them in the last chapter (how to distinguish social aggression from asocial violence) and we will cover the rest in Chapter Five (how to de-escalate a situation; how to use our social skills to avoid dangerous situations; how to let go of your ego, to apologize, to let the other guy have the parking space), but those answers don't satisfy them, either. What they want is something in between: a reliable way to stop the stabbing once the stabbing has started. A way to protect themselves against violence without having to use it. Sadly, there is no such thing. There is no "in between." If you want to prevent violence and avoid life-or-death situations, be smart and use your social skills to de-escalate, deflect, and disengage. If you want to *survive* violence once it's begun, to quote the poet Robert Frost, *the best way out is always through.* The only reliable path to survival is to use the very same tool of violence your attacker is trying to use against you, but to use it better.

In an ideal world, we'd be able to block our way to success—we could keep deflecting attacks until the aggressor gets tired and gives up. We could defend ourselves from violence without *really* using violence. I wish our world worked that way, but unfortunately it doesn't. It's a fantasy perpetuated by way too many bad self-defense classes. In the real world, I have learned that blocking, countering, "using his energy against him," and a whole host of other martial-arts-based techniques are all dangerous conceits that do little more than make us feel good about our relationship to violence—we feel prepared but we still get to wear the white hat—while doing almost nothing to solve the essential problem. They do nothing to shut down the attacker and degrade his ability to function. At best, such tactics delay the inevitable and ultimately give the other man free time and opportunity to carry out his work: injuring you and shutting you off.

To hammer this point home during my live training seminars, I will often bring two of my fellow instructors up on the mats and put them into a hypothetical knife-fight scenario. One instructor acts as the perpetrator with a rubber training knife. The other instructor is unarmed. We assume the person without the knife is facing an imminent threat, meaning the situation is asocial, he's devoid of choice, and there's no exit. He *must* act.

I tell the unarmed instructor to use a classic knife-defense maneuver—he's supposed to redirect the attack, control the knife, counter-attack, and attempt to take the knife away.

Then I tell the other instructor, "Your goal is to stab him to death. Ready? Go!"

I've conducted this demonstration time and again. Each time, I can see in the students' faces this sense of anticipatory relief like, "Okay great, finally I'm going to learn how the good guy—the guy without a weapon—can successfully escape a knife attack without getting hurt." It never works that way. It always goes horribly wrong. When my instructors go after each other at full speed, the bad guy always wins. He wins because he's acting, and the victim is only reacting. As the famous swordsman Miyamoto Musashi said, "You always grip the sword as if you want to kill a man."

This result bears itself out repeatedly in real knife assaults that have been caught on tape. Any victim who tries to protect themselves gets one, maybe two, deflections at most, before multiple successful stabbings by the perpetrator. It's a simple equation, really. On one side, we've given the good guy a stack of four things to execute. First, he has to redirect. Then he has to control. Then he has to counterattack. And finally, he has to take the knife away. That's a laundry list of tasks. On the other side of the equation, the perpetrator has only one directive: stab. Which approach is easier to execute?

I'll ask it a different way: do you know where doctors and police investigators find the most "defensive" wounds? On corpses. Simply put, executing violence is easier than defending against it.

Once the knife-wielding instructor finishes off the unarmed instructor (which usually happens very quickly) we run the demonstration back a second time except now we erase the list of defensive tasks for the unarmed instructor—the "good guy." We give him a new directive: don't defend, just injure. Inflict violence. End the other man.

When we run the demonstration this way, the results are

drastically different. The good guy realizes he must inflict injury quickly, so he's much more aggressive and direct with his actions. He's not thinking anymore. His mind is clear. He's not reacting, he's moving with intent. Now, even though the bad guy has a knife, the two men are more evenly matched, since they're each finally employing their greatest tactical advantage—a mindset with clarity and purpose. At that point, it's simply a race to first injury and then incapacitation.

Here's the truth: using real violence is binary. You're either doing it, or you're not. It's either on, or it's off. There is no middle ground, no halfway, no modulating levels of severity when it comes to protecting yourself in a life-or-death situation. You can't tear out someone's knee or stab them in the heart "just a little bit," any more than you can be a little bit dead or a little bit pregnant. It's all or nothing. Attempting to put degrees on violence by going easy or pulling punches only creates opportunities for your attacker to get to you first. Remember Diane and Sara from Chapter One? In the first scenario Diane learned the hard way that a minor laceration or contusion won't even slow down a dedicated person intent on doing you harm. And ask Sara about dealing with her dorm-room rapist. She'll tell you that you can't tear out someone's eye or crush their larynx with your forearm "just a little bit." It's all or nothing. Still, I can't tell you how often my students resist this idea and persist on trying to find a middle ground built on the empathy and humanity they assume is shared with their attackers. This mindset is the ultimate self-inflicted wound. As the great American journalist Ambrose Bierce once said, "We know what happens to people who stay in the middle of the road. They get run over."

Several years ago, a Los Angeles gangbanger was buying

groceries at a minimart in his neighborhood when a rival gang member walked in, spotted him, and pulled a gun. The man had just checked out at the cash register, which was at the end of an aisle on the opposite end of the store from the entrance. It was immediately clear to the gangbanger that there was no easy escape to be made. The only exit was through the aisles behind him and out the front door, where his armed rival now stood. Instinctively, the man understood that the only way he could tip things in his favor and survive the encounter was if he could close the distance, physically get his hands on his rival, and inflict an injury before the rival could zero in on him with his firearm. He was devoid of choice. He had to act. The only objects the gangbanger had at his disposal were the grocery bags in his hands, so he immediately threw them into the air and charged his rival, who began firing.

In the military, you learn that it's much harder to shoot somebody when they're charging at you. In battle, many casualties happen in overrun situations, when one side is *running away* and being pursued by the other, because the distance gives the pursuers more time to safely and accurately fire on the retreaters. It becomes a turkey shoot, in effect. The shopping gangbanger probably didn't learn his tactics in the military, but he understood how asocial violence worked well enough to immediately recognize the life-or-death situation in which he'd just been placed. He knew that if he was going to have any chance at survival he would have to run *toward* his enemy and inflict major injury. If he tried to hide, retreat, run away, or *defend,* his chances of survival would have dropped significantly. He knew that the only way out was through.

The man with the groceries absorbed five shots before plowing into the gunman. By closing the distance quickly, none of the shots could put him down or injure him to such an extent that he could not beat his rival to death with his fists, which he did.

"Good guys" need to learn what that gang member knew instinctively. There are no half-measures in life-or-death asocial violence. There is no bargaining or communication of any kind. There is only effective action with intent to injure and incapacitate. Whenever we take the victim's perspective, we're hobbling our minds and putting ourselves at a disadvantage. If we adopt the mindset of the aggressor, we flip the script and gain the edge. It starts by pulling yourself out of the victim's mindset, into the mindset of someone who, if necessary, is willing to fight—to *really fight*—to survive.

CAUSE STATE VS. EFFECT STATE: LANDING THE FIRST STRIKE

To change our mindset, we need to think about how we make decisions. I'll break down the decision-making process the same way I do for my students. It's also not a bad lesson for life in general: when you make a decision, you're either creating a new situation or reacting to an existing one. If you're creating a new situation, you're in *Cause State*. If you're reacting to an existing situation, you're in *Effect State*. In a life-or-death situation, you have to operate in Cause State all the time.

Consider the following scenario: You've been struck in the face, knocked to the ground, and most of your teeth are in your hand. You're on one knee and your assailant is standing over you preparing to kick you in the head to end it. There's a brief window. What do you do next?

The answer I'm looking for involves aggressive action. It doesn't involve retreating, or preparing to block, or figuring out what the perpetrator might do next. It doesn't involve yelling, either—unless that yelling happens in conjunction with some other major, significant action. If I've begun to successfully hardwire the proper programming into your mind, your first thought should be, "Where's my target? What can I do to inflict injury *right now?*" Like the gang-banger in the minimart, you need to go on offense. Whenever you find yourself in a situation of imminent danger, your thought process should always gravitate toward action, not reaction—toward cause, not effect.

This is not some novel concept. We understand the benefits of being proactive in every other aspect of our lives—in business, in relationships, in overcoming distractions—why shouldn't it also apply to violence and self-protection?

How often have you been derailed from a task by the vibration of your phone or an incoming email? These distractions pull you out of Cause State into Effect State, putting you in a reactive mode and taking you out of control of your situation. You know that you can, with practice and discipline, keep yourself in a proactive mode for longer and longer periods of time. You know that, when you're in Cause State, you act, get results, and reassess—you're not paralyzed and waiting for someone else to call the shots and act first.

There's only one way to get better at staying in Cause State: deliberately thinking about your decision-making process ahead of time. It allows you to react with speed and decisiveness. Speed and decisiveness aren't inborn character-istics for most of us—we have to learn them. Anybody can train themselves to behave this way, but like all training, physical or mental, the behaviors you want to build have to be practiced slowly, deliberately, and repeatedly, so that they are ingrained in your brain and ready to activate in the heat of the moment. So that they will come as second nature when you must execute at full speed.

In a pro basketball game, players don't react to forcing a turnover by stopping to think about what to do next. They automatically sprint to the other end of the court on a fast break, and if they act quickly enough, the sequence usually ends in an easy layup. No one is consciously processing information—everyone is operating at peak efficiency. They just *act*.

But how many times have they slowly and deliberately practiced that fast-break play? How many times have they prepared for the moment?

The very same principle—action, not reaction—applies in life-or-death situations. And the very same practice and discipline can help make it a part of our lives. In a life-or-death situation, a reactive response or lapse in focus can be fatal. Survival isn't the exclusive province of the bigger and stronger—it goes to the person who approaches his or her circumstances with the proper mindset, takes control of the situation and acts to cause decisive injury instead of reacting to the effects of someone else's choice.

Nowhere is the advantage of operating in Cause State clearer than in landing the first effective strike. When it comes to taking control of a violent situation, everything hinges on the initial injury. I've seen enough violent confrontations play out to know that the struggle is balanced on a knife edge until someone gets a debilitating injury, at which point the situation shifts strongly in the favor of the person who was successful. Everything after that is academic, because inflicting the initial injury is a way of permanently consigning your enemy to Effect State.

What does that mean in practice? It means that you want to be the first one to inflict debilitating injury, and you want to do it as quickly as possible. When you realize you're in a fight for your life, don't waste time making an elaborate strategy or waiting to see what your opponent is going to do, because whatever you worry about is the thing that is most likely to happen. If you're worried he'll hit you, he will. If you're worried he'll counterattack, he will. If you're worried he'll kill you — he's a lot more likely to. The brain will do whatever you tell it to do. By worrying about the attacker, you're telling it to focus in what is fundamentally an Effect State, rather than a Cause State, which requires much clearer direction: "Throat!"; "Eyes!"; "Knee!" If you focus on that, on *action,* you are more likely to be successful. And then things simplify all by themselves.

Put the idea of an assessment phase out of your mind. There is no dropping into a fighting stance. There is no waiting to block or counter. Those are parts of the Effect State — the defensive mindset — and that will get you killed. If you can "put your dukes up" in defense, waiting to see what your attacker does first, you can use the same motion to be proactive once you see your first, best opportunity and put your fingers into your enemy's eyes or your forearm through his neck (like Sara did, and she never had a chance to put *her* dukes up). Don't waste that motion by going halfway. Like the gangbanger in the minimart or Jorge Orozco, take that motion and put it through your attacker and break something inside of him. Violence isn't chess at ninety miles per hour. It's demolition derby. And just like demolition derby, it's the driver with the most forward momentum who usually wins.

CONTROLLING YOUR INTENT

There is no substitute for inflicting debilitating injury. It turns a life-or-death situation in your favor. It transforms an awful, scary man into an injured man, helpless to keep you from escaping to safety or causing further harm to fully neutralize him.

What kind of person can inflict a debilitating injury in self-defense? Let me describe them for you: they're not timid, they don't dance around, they don't worry about being countered or even killed—they just plow in with clear intent, like the result is a foregone conclusion, focused above all on causing that injury and not stopping until it's achieved. They are you, with an action-first mindset and a clear understanding of the tool of violence.

Some people just call this attitude "confidence," while others call it an "offensive mindest" or "aggression." I call it *intent*. As in, "intent to cause harm," because that is the cleanest, simplest way to describe the actions of the winners in every knife fight, prison yard fight, convenience store hold-up, and bar fight I have analyzed over the last twenty-five years. It's precisely what my fellow instructors and I try to instill in our clients when we train: we get out on the mats and look for targets to smash with no hesitation or reactivity. When we get out on the mats, we simulate hurting one another, not blocking or warding off attacks. When it's your turn to go, my goal is for that action-first, injury-first, Cause State mindset to trigger and for you to plow through the vulnerable target we've exposed for you.* The first thing that hops out of you should be an attempt to cause an injury that produces debilitating trauma and breakage that shuts down your enemy's command center before he can shut down yours.

What exactly do you need to practice to be confident in delivering incapacitating injuries? There is no magic series of "moves" or "techniques"—later, I'll explain why those concepts are exactly the wrong way to think about self-protection. What you need to practice, most of all, is *intent*. You need to appreciate the value of intent to cause debilitating injury, you need to control it, and you need to activate it at the right moment, when you're in a fight for your life.

Intent is the filter through which mindset turns into action. For most people who find themselves in a life-or-death confrontation, their intent will be to flee, or worse, to try and weather the storm until help magically arrives. Even after going through training, some of my students will feel their intent slip into flight, instead of fight, when given scenarios to game out. They'll channel their adrenaline rush into a burst of energy that gets them as far away from a dangerous situation as possible—a good response in scenarios of social aggression, but a disastrous one in precisely the kind of situations we're training for, the asocial ones in which flight is impossible.

---

* Training to injure is covered in depth in Chapter Nine.

How can that be, after so much focus on mindset training? Weren't they paying attention? Of course they were. The problem is, *you can't fake intent.* You can know the intent you're supposed to have, and I can lecture to you until I'm blue in the face and you're bored to tears, but if you don't have it, then you will end up going through the motions of violence, and they will be half-hearted, limp, and all but useless. Fully committing to and controlling the intent to inflict injury is essential to decisively shutting down the body of an aggressor trying to take your life — even one who is many times bigger, stronger, and scarier than you.

You can have years of "training," but if you lack the intent, you'll lose every time. Intent is what makes people scary: it's what you fear in a criminal, and it's what a criminal must fear in you. And you develop your intent by practicing the kinds of attacks to the kinds of targets that, in real life, result in debilitating injury. It's not the real thing—no simulation is—but it's as close as you can get, and we will cover that in depth in Part 2.

EMBRACE THE UGLY

In the end, this is why there's no such thing as "self-defense"— there's no protecting yourself in a life-or-death fight without being willing to use the very same tool of violence that your adversary wants to use against you. People who survive such encounters do so because they have the mindset and the intent it takes to do real harm to another human being when real harm is what's required—either because that mindset was ingrained in them all along, or, more realistically, because they deliberately cultivated it through training.

I know that this is an unsentimental, unromantic, even brutal lesson about violence. I am asking you to embrace the ugly, to think about violence in this pragmatic way, because that is precisely how your enemy thinks. To defeat him, you need to think like he does. Make no mistake, for the purposes of saving your life—or someone else's life—I am asking you to mentally prepare yourself to think like a criminal when the situation calls for it. That doesn't mean I'm teaching you to *become* a criminal. I am just depriving the criminal of their asymmetric mental edge over you. These mental tools don't turn off an empathy switch when they are in the hands of good people like you. Learning how to use the tool of violence doesn't just *make* you a violent criminal, just as learning to use a hammer for carpentry doesn't *make* you use it for assault, or learning to drive a truck doesn't *make* you steer it into a bunch of tourists on the streets of Nice.

But learning how to use the tool of violence does mean using criminals' own techniques against them, to debilitate and neutralize them, when the choice to de-escalate has been removed and there is no exit in sight. That means that, whether we like it or not, we have a lot to learn from the bad guys.

CHAPTER FOUR

THE WORST PEOPLE HAVE THE BEST INFORMATION

Good people exasperate one's reason; bad people stir one's imagination.

—*Oscar Wilde*

The prison system is a petri dish of asocial violence. It is a Darwinian proving ground for many of the ideas I have shared with you so far: stepping through your opponent, the natural disadvantage of assuming a victim's mentality, the intent to injure first and fastest, a bias always toward action, disinterest in judgments about violence beyond whether it is effective. My career in self-protection training has taken me to some amazing places all over the world, but it has been my deep study of the tool of violence and my search for uncomfortable truths like these, that has taken me to a place few ever go: the American prison system.

In civilized society, the economy runs on money and credit. In the prison system, the baseline currency is the effective use of criminal violence. In society, the wealthiest people have the most money and the best credit. In prison, the wealthiest people are the most effective practitioners of violence. In society, you can survive being broke. You can get by. In a maximum-security prison, that notion is a non-starter. You cannot survive without access to and an accumulation of the basic currency—the effective use of violence. In prison, to paraphrase the rapper 50 Cent, you either get rich or die trying.

Through my work with correctional officers and law enforcement agencies, I have been able to study case reports and security camera footage from countless prison yard and cellblock confrontations. Many of the important lessons I have learned and will share in this book came from those videos, from the men and women featured in them who have not just survived in the prison system, but thrived. They are members of prison gangs, predators, violent criminals. By societal standards, they are the worst of us. By prison standards, they are the best. But in watching one video in particular, I learned something else; something that deepened and crystallized my understanding of the criminal element and their relationship to violence. I was sitting with a correctional officer and he was cueing up video of fights in the yard and the dining hall in the prison where he worked for me to review. They were standard fare, as these things go, and we discussed them with a similarly low level of enthusiasm. Then the officer perked up, as if he'd just remembered something, and told me about a video from earlier that morning that I *had* to watch.

The corrections officer cued up a short clip on his computer monitor that showed two men standing across from each other. They weren't fighting—which is what I was expecting to see—but they *were* practicing stabbing techniques. It didn't look like anything you'd see in an MMA cage or a boxing gym. One guy was slowly simulating a striking motion into the other. It looked like a stabbing motion, but it was slow and methodical, from strange angles that didn't seem like they would be very effective.

This was not a typical approach to stabbing someone—it wasn't like anything I learned in hand-to-hand combat training in the military, or that I'd seen in any of the hundreds of other prison videos I've watched. The prisoner mimicking an attack wasn't targeting the spleen, liver, neck, or even the upper chest area where people are typically trained to strike with a knife. He was stabbing different areas of the torso, at different angles of entry.

The officer looked at me and asked, "Any idea what they're doing?"

"It looks like some sort of training, but it's strange. I've never seen these techniques before."

"Yeah. It's definitely different," he said, goading me into the obvious next question.

"What is it?" I asked. "Is it some weird type of martial art?"

"No," the officer replied. "Yesterday we had an incident in the yard that brought the CERT team out.* This was the first time they'd been activated since we got in a whole new body armor configuration. The prisoners knew it had come in, so they staged a fight to get their first look at it."

"Did they really?" I asked. "That's pretty calculating."

---

* CERT stands for Correctional Emergency Response Team. It's the prison version of a SWAT team.

"What you are looking at is two members of the Black Guerrilla Family simulating how and where to stab the most vulnerable gaps in our new armor.* They're locking that info in right now. Each of these angles you're seeing—they can get a shank in and penetrate us through our armor in those locations. That was the only reason they staged the incident yesterday—so the rest of them could get a detailed look at the armor and find the weaknesses."

Neither of the two men training in the video were in great shape and, according to the corrections officer, they weren't particularly brilliant, either. Despite media's insistence on depicting violent criminals as huge, fearsome, ripped juggernauts, these were your run-of-the-mill prisoners—as were most of the men who orchestrated and participated in the staged fight. Yet they were savvy enough to have conducted what amounts to a reconnaissance mission, then debriefed, processed the learnings, and organized it into a loose training protocol, all in less than twenty-four hours.

It was eye-opening. There has never been a doubt in my mind that the prison system houses many of the most skilled practitioners of hand-to-hand combat, or combat with improvised weapons, but what I realized from this video was that the reason they are so skilled is because *they have the best information, and they know how to use it,* despite, by and large, having zero formal training in combat sports or martial arts.

---

* The Black Guerilla Family is a notorious African-American prison gang founded in the mid-1960s at San Quentin Prison. A Black Guerilla Family member killed Black Panther leader, Huey Newton, on the streets of Oakland, California, in 1989.

DOWN TO BUSINESS

When it comes to violence, one of the most unsettling things for people about learning from criminals is reckoning with the sober, workman-like nature of how they skillfully deploy brutality. It's disconcerting for it to seem so...easy. We want to believe that there is something innate and exceptional in these men, something coded into their DNA, that makes them better at violence than everyone else. Sure, we're all wired biologically and evolutionarily to use violence effectively, but we feel like there's something *in the marrow* with these guys. They're a different breed.

The reality is, what makes criminals better at violence is that they don't romanticize it—they treat it like it's business. In my time interviewing high-ranking prison gang members while also training business executives in self-protection, I've continually noticed parallels between the two worlds. They're both very savvy and possess all the different kinds of intelligence that help them succeed. They both have clear goals and act with purpose. They both value precise, timely execution. And neither of them have time for opinions or sentiment—they only want facts.

In business, there are always a million threats to your success. Someone is always gunning for you and oftentimes it's someone you weren't expecting. The players who thrive are the ones who have the most, best information, who know all the most effective and efficient ways to leverage that information to their objectives, who have trained or studied or practiced methodically and gotten their ten thousand hours in, so to speak, and who have cultivated the right mindset to make the right move when a deal is about to fall apart or the company is hanging in the balance.

This is exactly what the two Black Guerilla Family members were doing in the video taken out in the yard. In the same way that you might take a class to learn how to do pivot tables in Microsoft Excel or attend a seminar from an expert, they were teaching themselves classes in an important part of their profession: the business of injuring and killing. They'd acquired the best, most up-to-date information the day before from the staged fight. They'd learn the best ways to use it by examining the CERT team's new gear, and now they were training effective movements deliberately, over and over, to sear them into their brains so they could call on them like muscle memory at a moment's notice.

Their surprisingly methodical training process compelled me to take a closer look at the rest of the videos I saw that day. And I'm so glad I did, because I found a similar mindset at work in every violent event I watched. In one of the most telling videos I watched, it wasn't the combatants themselves who caught my eye; it was the audience. As a violent confrontation developed, everyone would crowd around and watch—a perfectly normal reaction, even outside of prison. But the similarities ended there. The facial expressions and body language of the spectators were unlike anything you'd find with people who were there for entertainment or to witness a power struggle within the social hierarchy. The men surrounding these prison yard fights looked like people who were there to learn. Their faces were steady and serious. They were watching almost clinically, studying the fight and taking mental notes: what worked and what didn't, where did the outcome of the fight turn, which one of these guys was going to be the bigger threat in the future. They were doing *research,* cataloging information for their own use the next time they found (or put) themselves in a life-or-death scenario.

To survive in prison is not unlike winning in business, so it should be no surprise that the way gang members use violence as a currency is the same way entrepreneurs use capital. It's a commodity that gives them leverage and power— one they can't afford to take for granted or use carelessly. They must be judicious and exacting, with a laser focus on using it to their advantage and getting results, while also being prepared to make big bets and go all in.

One of the ways they use that capital most effectively is in securing all the help they can get, whether that means personnel or matériel. They don't go it alone if they don't have to. If you get into a car accident and the other driver sues you for all you're worth, for instance, you're not going to represent yourself. You're going to retain the services of a lawyer who hopefully knows everything there is to know about car accidents and liability laws, who has a ton of trial experience, and a reputation for winning. An attorney with expertise in a different area might be cheaper or nicer or a friend of a friend, but choosing him is just going to increase the chance that you lose your case. Common sense, right? Yet, when it comes to violence, to fighting off another person who wants to take you for everything you're worth— *your life*—we struggle with the notion that a violent criminal could be our best friend, or that we could learn something from the world they inhabit. Instead, we close our eyes, stick our fingers in our ears, and turn away—whether it's news footage of a prison riot, dash cam footage of a convict attacking a police officer, or simply the mental imagery I am creating in these pages.

The problem with that mindset is that regular exposure (and practice) is the only way to learn a new skill or ingrain a new mindset. Whenever you're learning something new—whether it's tying your shoes or learning how to fight a criminal—there's no substitute for actual experience, for seeing and hearing and doing it. Prisoners exist in a world where violence is a regular occurrence and the threat of violence is a constant. They have unmatched exposure to and experience in real, life-or-death violence. They not only learn from true experts—each other—they partake in real-world training. They live and breathe the stuff. That's the crucial advantage they have over the rest of us, who are almost always insulated from real violence—and that's why we have to learn from them. We can't look away and pretend it doesn't exist; we must strip away the emotion and the moral judgments and evaluate the violent events we encounter in our lives with the laser focus and clinical precision of inmates around a fight.

It is not the most comfortable idea to wrap your hands around, to be sure, but we often get life-saving information from ugly places. Doctors learn how to protect and save the human body by dissecting corpses. Workplace safety regulations are born of the study of workplace accidents. Seatbelts, airbags, and crumple zones were designed by deconstructing thousands of fatal car wrecks. Like the open road and the factory floor, the prison system is also the best source of real world information about how to use and protect against violence. In prison, there are no weight classes. There's no boxing ring. There are no rules of engagement. The premium is on creativity and unpredictability...and success. These are the same conditions you'll face if you're confronted with violence out in the real world (or competition in the business world). Let us not dismiss out of hand the good lessons that come from bad people when the stakes are so high.

THE ONE ON THE GROUND IS THE ONE *IN* THE GROUND

In the last chapter I showed you an image of two figures locked in a violent struggle. I explained how criminals never see themselves as the guy being choked. I mentioned how some of the guys I talked to even suggested how they would do things better.

One of those guys was a prison gang enforcer in the same medium-security facility as the Black Guerilla Family members who were planning ways to circumvent the guards' new body armor. I'll call this man Damon. What Damon told me he would do different tactically isn't important for our discussion here, but he told me some things about his mindset that were revealing.

Damon told me that even when he is at a disadvantage in a real fight, he only sees himself as the attacker, *the standing man.* Even when he's losing the fight—in his own mind, he is *never* the one on the ground. Even when he is *actually* on the ground, fully horizontal, even if he's been ambushed and his survival is teetering on the knife's edge, his mind has a way of tilting the image on its side. Now the winner is lying on his back and the loser is above him. Regardless of the orientation, he always sees himself as the one doing the damage. Thus, he is just as comfortable and ready to inflict lethal injury upside-down, in the air, or pinned to the floor as he is standing up with his feet planted firmly in the ground. He has to feel that way, otherwise he's dead. Or as he puts it:

If you think you're the guy on the ground, you'll end up being the guy in *the ground.*

Identifying with the downed man is to identify with the loser, the victim, the one getting done in. In the zero-sum nature of the prison experience, that means identifying with the dead. And in this world—a system of complicated power relationships and rigid hierarchies that sit on a foundation of asocial violence—anyone who thinks that way creates a self-fulfilling prophecy.

This is how Damon has survived the many who have wanted him dead over the decades. This is why his demeanor is chillingly calm and relaxed. When we spoke, Damon never got excited or emotional. When he narrated what he would have done differently as the dominant man in the training image, or when he recounted any number of his own violent confrontations, they were not dramatic re-enactments so much as calculated reconstructions. He spoke matter-of-factly, without the veneer of machismo. He told me that the moment he stops thinking and acting clearly and directly, he's as good as dead.

In a normal social context, we might call this mindset "evil," or, if we're being more clinical, "pathological." But we're not talking about normal situations here. We're talking about life-or-death situations. In that context, Damon's mindset is simply utilitarian. The trick for us sane and socialized folk is to keep such points of view confined to the realm of asocial violence and not let them become—as they have for Damon the prison gang enforcer—a way of life. Either way, we have at least one thing in common with Damon. Our perspective dictates our actions—no matter how much we wish otherwise.

If we can remember that, then when the time comes we can accomplish the same goal that Damon has for many years: to stay off the ground, so we don't end up *in* the ground.

THE WAR FACE

Whenever I watch a video that captures an instance of deadly violence, whether in prison or on the streets, I try to get a look at the attacker's face. Not because I want to identify him—I'm not a criminal investigator. I'm looking for something more basic.

Our experience with media, sports, and gamified violence* tells us to expect to find some kind of "war face" on the aggressor. You know what I'm talking about: that intimidating, terrifying visage filled with fury, with eyes bugged out, brow furrowed, and teeth bared. It's the kind of face that communicates a social message: "Do not mess with me."

You will rarely if ever see that face on a real killer. A real killer does not want to communicate anything with anyone. He has no interest in frightening anyone, or telling you how angry he is. He doesn't care whether you think he's serious. He does not have a message to send. He just wants to injure his targets as badly as he can. He wants to shut off a human brain. It's a focused, action-first mindset with clear, singular intent.

I often have to tell my students and clients to stop messing around with their facial expressions during training

---

* We will talk about gamified violence in Chapter Five.

exercises. When I see people making the angry face as they engage a target, I know they're really afraid. The angry face is their attempt to cover it up. In a simulation on the mats, they might be able to fool their training partner, but really they're not fooling anyone but themselves. And they *certainly* aren't fooling a truly violent predator. A real lion doesn't roar when she goes in for the kill. Those loud, angry displays are for show—the epitome of social aggression.

Watching criminals commit violence has taught me that there's only one reliable way to determine intent, and it's not by looking at their face, but by examining how they interface with their targets. Those who are most effective at teaching and practicing self-protection can tap into this kind of intent when they need to, not by making a scary face, but just by getting the work done.

Recently, I organized a demonstration for some new students in San Diego. I asked Andy, an instructor, and Kevin, an advanced student, to roll through some free fighting to show all the students where their blows are supposed to land. Andy was absolutely savaging Kevin (as often happens when instructors are on stage and really push things for maximum benefit to the students), delivering a simulated beating that was both brilliant and ugly at the same time, doing things I'd never seen (or dreamed of) before. I felt the warmth of a predator's appreciation.

And then I looked at Andy's face.

In the midst of all that furious action—arms and legs going in every direction—Andy's face was the singular dead spot. Flat. Slack. He looked, for want of a better term, bored. Only his eyes were alive, intent on each target in rapid succession.

While it warmed my heart to see such perfect execution, I could only imagine what such an apparent incongruity looked like to the uninitiated students surrounding them on the mat. Chilling, probably. It was the face of a killer— emotionless, done without talk, here now for the purpose of violence only as long as necessary.

To the initiated, Andy's face says far more about violence and the intentional infliction of injury than the angry face ever could. I would never have learned what that face meant unless I spent time in prisons. And while prison is probably the best place to find information about real violence, there are a few other places where we can learn from our enemies— including combat.

WHAT OUR ENEMIES KNOW

As a private contractor instructing hand-to-hand combat, I've spent a lot of time with special forces units. Once, I was speaking with the senior officer of a SEAL team, who told me about a vehicle convoy training exercise he had just completed. In Afghanistan and Iraq, the primary offensive strategy employed by Al-Qaeda and Taliban fighters are ambushes built around IEDs planted on roadways that U.S. troops use to move men and matériel. As you might imagine, that makes convoy protection a big deal. The senior officer created an exercise that would put the troops into a simulated ambush situation where they would have to fight their way out while securing the convoy.

As an experiment, he ran the exercise in two different ways—first with conventional troops, then with highly trained special operations units. Here's what he found: across the board, the special forces teams, including the SEALs, performed no better than the conventional troops when it came to dealing with ambushes. Neither special operations training, nor elite physical fitness, were adequate protection from an ambush for even our military's most elite units—and, of course, our enemies understand this well.

The question we need to ask ourselves is, *why?* What is the tactical advantage built into an ambush that makes it so difficult to defend against? Simply put: by definition, an ambush is about seizing the initiative. That alone neutralizes the advantage of even the most elite adversaries. By seizing the initiative, you put yourself in Cause State and force your opponent to react, keeping them off balance, in Effect State. In Effect State, pretty much everyone—from ordinary grunts to elite SEALs—performs the same: poorly. Which should tell you that: 1) *everyone* is susceptible to violence in the Effect State, and 2) the best defense isn't defense at all, it's offense.

Training exercises like this SEAL ambush drill and the knife-attack demonstration I have my instructors conduct with our students are good tools for introducing the principles of real world violence, but nothing is quite as instructive as those principles born out in real life.

In 2003, a security guard at a Walmart in Ukiah, California, caught an eighteen-year-old female shoplifter trying to make her way out the door with a couple hundred dollars in merchandise. He apprehended her, detained her in the security office, and called the local police.

Ukiah Police Sergeant Marcus Young responded to the call. He took the report from the security guard, then escorted the perpetrator to his patrol car parked out front. As he was putting her into his police car, he noticed a small male walking toward him. He was wearing a hooded sweatshirt and both hands were in his pockets.

Sergeant Young was a seventeen-year veteran, former military trainer, and a highly skilled martial artist. He was a decorated police officer. He immediately recognized that something was strange about the hooded man, so he yelled out a command: "Stop. Show me your hands." The man kept approaching. "Show me your hands!" As the man got within striking distance, he pulled a knife from his pocket. Sergeant Young knew the guy was too close to stop with a firearm at that point, so he swiftly executed a double wrist-turn knife disarm, grasping and twisting the man's wrists to loosen his grip on the knife. That's what he was trained to do, and it worked perfectly. He felt the man's wrist snap as he twisted and turned with all his might.

There was only one problem. From the other pocket, the man pulled a five-round revolver, emptying all five rounds into Sergeant Young. Two bullets lodged in Sergeant Young's body armor, but the others pierced his hand, arm, back, and cheek. Young dropped to the ground. As he lay on the ground bleeding profusely, the Walmart security guard leapt onto the hooded man's back, knocking him away from Young. The hooded man casually let the empty firearm go, transferred the knife from his bad hand to his good hand, and stabbed the Walmart guard twice.

On what should have been a routine call, Sergeant Young brought a seventeen-year-old police cadet along. During the initial confrontation, the cadet was on the radio calling for backup. But now, with Young on the ground partially paralyzed by the gunshots, and his hooded attacker making a beeline for the shotgun and AR-15 racked inside the open patrol car, backup was useless. Young called the unarmed cadet over and told him to unholster Young's weapon, which was on his right hip, and transfer it to his left hand—the only one that was still working. Just in time, Sergeant Young somehow found enough strength to fix his aim and pull the trigger, fatally shooting the attacker just as he was about to grab the AR-15 rifle.

Both Sergeant Young and the Walmart security guard survived their wounds. And when people read their story, they always talk about how Sergeant Young's heroic actions saved their lives.[*]

The praise is well deserved, but there's something more to be learned from this story. Both Young and the Walmart guard were trained to go after the enemy's tools, but the enemy knew that the tools are not really what matters. What matters is the mindset that controls intent and the internal command center—the brain—that controls everything else. By focusing only on the tools the man was using, the knife and gun, the two men didn't fully account for the hooded man's true weapon—his brain. They didn't attempt anything, like a strike to the neck or to the temple, that could create concussion and shut off his brain. As a result, they were unprepared to deal with his singular intent and mental drive, which resulted in a failure to lock down the threat.

---

[*] "Officer Down: The Marcus Young Incident," LawOfficer.com, June 2, 2010, lawofficer.com/archive/officer-down-the-marcus-young-incident.

They were more concerned with disarming than incapacitating, and in this case, it cost them severely. They were so focused, in each case, on just one of the weapons the attacker had, which was how they ended up on the receiving end of the other. Their enemy wasn't thinking that way. He was focused on a deadly mission, and that's why he nearly won a two-on-one altercation.

How, then, do we take out the enemy's command center? We'll talk about this more in Chapter Seven, but for now, just keep this in mind: the goal is to produce enough trauma to trigger a spinal reflex reaction, which causes the body to focus on the injury. When the brain is focused on injury, it can't perform any other actions. It's impossible for a person in the throes of that kind of reaction to plan, to make decisions, or to think about *anything* other than the trauma.

We've all experienced it, at least in small doses. You feel it when you step on a sharp object, like a tack or a nail. Your foot automatically comes up, and your mind freezes. Or when you touch a hot surface, your hand automatically recoils—and again, you can't think about anything else. Before there's even a thought in your head, your body reacts, because the nervous system kicks in. The stimulus goes up the spinal cord and your brain takes urgent action to protect your body from further trauma—at the expense of temporarily shutting down conscious processing. You're no longer acting. You're reacting.

In the case of Sergeant Young and the Walmart guard, neither one of them delivered enough trauma to end the threat from the hooded man, to shut off his brain. And he made them pay for it.

THE MEXICAN MAFIA'S REQUIRED READING LIST

A teacher hands you three books for a new class: Machiavelli's *The Prince,* Robert Greene's *48 Laws of Power,* and Robert Comer's *Abnormal Psychology.*

What do you think the class is about? Maybe something related to political science. Possibly a class about how revolutions start? Heck, it could be a survey course on the creation of American presidents.

Then the teacher gives you three more books. You don't recognize any of the titles, but they're all about human anatomy. Now what do you think this class is about?

In fact, this is a prison syllabus. An informal one, but no less real. In a recorded interview from inside prison, a notorious Mexican Mafia leader explained how he developed the education process for senior members of his organization. It began with a specific list of books—including those I just mentioned—and a set of subjects that were considered required reading for his lieutenants, on the inside and the outside. His list was as long as the one given to special forces officers at the JFK Center at Fort Bragg. The content was only slightly different. The major difference was the mafia leader's focus on human anatomy. It was the dominant subject on the reading list, by far. It formed the gang's blueprint for success in using the tool of violence.

The emphasis on anatomy is about expediency. The mafia leader knows that with guards, cameras, and rivals everywhere, a member he sanctions to conduct a hit often will only get one shot. If his lieutenant doesn't kill his rival successfully, without being seen, he'll likely be moved into protective custody or even transferred to another facility. That would be a huge blow to the organization, so he needs to ensure a swift and effective strike to a vital region of the target's body. And the way to do that is to have a thorough understanding of how the body responds to trauma.

This focus is not unique to the Mexican Mafia, of course. Every major gang that I've studied—the Aryan Brotherhood, the Mexican Mafia, the Black Guerrilla Family—has an edict that members in the upper echelons must study anatomy. They've all composed reading lists like the one the Mexican Mafia leader relayed to his prison interrogator.

In the course of my research, I once examined a set of seemingly innocuous letters sent from a recently released prisoner to a gang member who was entering jail for the first time. It turns out the letters were coded. When you decode them, you find that the content is all about applying violence to human targets: how to make a shank, where to stab most efficiently, and how to inflict injury on another person in the event of a brawl. It was all precise, specific, and to the point.

It makes sense, right? These gangs are all in the same business—the business of violence. Violence is the source of their power. It's the currency that gives them power over prisons, streets, and drug distribution. When doing harm to human bodies is a key part of your job description, a detailed understanding of the human body is a requirement for staying in business.

This focus on anatomy is a major clue about how to use the tool of violence. Criminals don't look at *bigger, faster,* or *stronger.* They look at the human body—most important, the weaknesses that every human body has in common. I've seen a 5'7", 145-pound gangster take out a 6'6", 240-pound Aryan

Brother by jumping into him, stabbing him in the eye, and then continuing to stab him in other areas until he died.

It wasn't one of the giant Mongol biker regulars at Jose Murphy's that took out my bouncer buddy Mike back in the '80s; it was the small, squirrelly guy off to the side with the blade in his boot and years of prison time on his résumé. His survival on the inside undoubtedly depended on his ability to even the playing field against guys who held a physical advantage. Knowing exactly where to strike is the first step, because while circumstances will always be different, anatomy never is. Mike's Achilles tendon and femoral artery were in the same place on his body as every other man in that bar.

If you look at somebody bigger, faster, and stronger and immediately think, "I'm at a disadvantage," I have news for you: you are. But that's only because you just put yourself there for no reason.

The truth is that anyone can do debilitating violence to anyone else. Your size, your speed, your strength, your gender—all the factors that untrained people *think* make the difference when it comes to violence—all matter far less than your mindset and your intent. And anyone can cultivate those. The tools to protect yourself against lethal violence are much more accessible than you think. You don't have to earn a black belt or put on an extra fifty pounds of muscle. You do have to learn about the vulnerabilities that make all human bodies equal, and you do have to build the intent to take advantage of those vulnerabilities in time to save your life.

Never think "I'm at a disadvantage." Instead, think, "How close am I to his throat? Can I get to his knee? Or his groin? Or his eye?" It was this precise mindset that saved Sara's life in her dorm room bunk and neutralized the disadvantageous position she and her roommate had placed themselves in as targets. That's how to flip things in your favor. When you understand anatomy, you strip the opponent's power down to almost nothing.

THINK LIKE YOUR OPPONENT

I know the stories we've covered in this chapter have the potential to be quite jarring. Their main characters—prison inmates and violent criminals—are frightening people who are neither admirable nor inspirational. But for one, very specific objective—fighting for your life in violent situations that you cannot de-escalate or escape—they *are* good role models.

"How is that a good thing?!" you're probably asking yourself.

Their lessons—attacking rather than retreating, directly incapacitating the human body by shutting off the brain, and understanding the human body's inherent weak points—may be unpleasant or counterintuitive. But in situations of life-or-death violence, this is how your opponent is already thinking—and if that's how *they* are thinking, that's how *you* have to think, as well. If you can wrap your head around why it works, you can learn how to use it to your advantage. And you will quickly come to realize that it is the most effective means of protecting yourself.

The rules of asocial violence are very simple: don't make yourself a target, focus your mind, know the human body, act first, intend to injure, don't stop until he's incapacitated or dead. It's black and white versus social aggression's infinite shades of gray. No one knows these rules better than the people who have defined them; the prisoners and predators who got very good at violence by learning from what you might call real-world, on-the-job training with true experts — each other.

There is no substitute for that kind of practice. But since our goal is for you to never have to practice this stuff in real life, I will settle for knowing that you have all the information bad guys have and that you are able to think how they think.

Just don't make the mistake of judging them based on their crimes. Judge them based on whether they are still alive, because that's the goal for all of us.

CHAPTER FIVE

WHEN VIOLENCE ISN'T THE ANSWER

A strange game. The only winning move is not to play.
— *WarGames*, 1983

Until the first injury is inflicted, violence is always a coin flip, no matter how justified you are in using it. You take on those odds when you're fighting for your life, just as when you're stupidly escalating a confrontation you should have walked away from. My goal, up to this point, has been to demystify violence as an idea and deprogram your moral judgments about it as a tool, so that you will be less likely to hesitate in assuming the risks of action under those rare asocial circumstances where the alternative to action is death. But because the risks of life-or-death violence are so high, and because the outcome is so unpredictable, it's also wise to better understand the nature of social aggression and to think in terms of violence *prevention:* strategies that can keep you from getting into confrontations that don't need to happen and from having to fight for your life in confrontations that weren't your choice.

The entire premise of this book is that violence is rarely the answer, but for some questions, it is the *only* answer. And yet I also believe that there are many ways to test out of ever being asked these questions in the first place. If properly vigilant, one can often avoid being forced to answer altogether. Of course, I'm not the first person to think that way.

In 1736, Benjamin Franklin organized America's first fire department—The Union Fire Company of Philadelphia. Franklin was acting in response to a devastating fire along the city's waterfront in 1730 and the city council's decision in the wake of the destruction to buy three new pumpers (the single pumper they had in 1730 was utterly useless), four hundred water buckets, and a bunch of other gear... *without also organizing and training men to use them.* The year before he formed the fire company, Franklin wrote a letter to the editor of the *Pennsylvania Gazette* (a newspaper he owned) under a pseudonym, admonishing the city council for its refusal to train the citizenry in basic firefighting techniques that could save many lives.

"An ounce of prevention," he counseled Philadelphia's leaders, "is worth a pound of cure."

This phrase has become one of Franklin's most famous quotes, probably because it applies to so many things in life. Self-protection is no exception. Most of this book is about cure—and not just a pound of it, *a ton of it*—because my goal is to prepare you for the blazing inferno of life-or-death violence. But that's not enough. Sometimes the inferno is too powerful. Sometimes it is of our own making. And even for those of us who are best prepared, who are able to fight for our lives and win, there's something far better: never having to fight for our lives at all. Think of the rest of this chapter as fire-retardant.

I would be thrilled if you never had to use any of the self-protection methods I teach in this book—ever. I would love it if I were put out of business because people were smart, because they were aware and prepared, because they implement the simple, small strategies that can make a remarkable difference in keeping violence out of their lives. I would love it because I know what it looks like when people aren't smart and go about their lives oblivious and unprepared. It's not pretty.

THE THREE-DAY TEST

We've been thinking mostly about confrontations that *others* escalate into the realm of real, life-or-death violence, violence without communication and without rules. But what if *we're the ones* thinking about escalating a confrontation? What if we have found ourselves on the short end of a bully–victim dynamic and enough is enough? How do we know if it's worth it? (Hint: it's never worth it.)

It's very simple:

Three days from now, if you're sitting in a jail cell or lying in a pine box, was the escalation worth it?

You have to ask yourself that question, you have to consider the worst-case scenario, because once you choose to escalate a conflict, that's where things can very well end up. It's why I treat every new person I meet like they're six seconds away from opening fire. Once you choose the tool of violence, you lose control of the outcome. Trust me: in my seminars, I've had more than one client who got run off the road, who confronted the other drivers, and were beaten to within an inch of their lives—and who had no idea that they'd end up in such horribly destructive situations, even though they were the ones who initially responded with aggression. It doesn't matter whether they were sticking up for themselves, or whether they were in the right at the beginning—to a man, they'll tell you it wasn't worth it, because the tool of violence doesn't care who's in the right when it gets picked up, it only cares who swings it best.

There was a famous Muay Thai fighter named Alex Gong, who lived in San Francisco. He was an amazing competitor, and he always worked out at his gym by the Golden Gate Bridge. One day, when a couple of his students were taking a break outside, a car came barreling down the street, pulled into the gym's parking lot to turn around, and side-swiped Alex's car. The driver sped away from the accident and back onto the main road, but he quickly got caught in traffic.

Alex's students ran back into the gym to tell him what had happened. "Alex! Somebody just hit your car and we can still see him! He's stuck in traffic." Alex was enraged. He jumped out of the ring with his gloves and gear still on and ran down the street toward the car. When he found the culprit, he started banging on the window and yelling aggressively—"Hey, asshole! You hit my car!"

Picture that: a trained, sweaty Muay Thai fighter in his fighting gear, making loud threats and aggressively trying to break a car's window. The ordinary driver's reaction would most likely be fear and panic. But this was no ordinary driver on the other side of the glass—this was an escaped felon.

He had stolen his girlfriend's car and was trying to flee the area because he knew he'd soon be pursued by law enforcement. He had taken a wrong turn, frantically realized his mistake, and turned around in Alex's parking lot. De-escalation and talking his way out of trouble were not in the cards for this man. Very quickly this had become a zero-sum game. Without a word in response to Alex's threats and gesticulations, the driver lifted a .45 caliber handgun to the window and shot Alex twice in the chest.*

Alex was a powerful fighter, but that didn't matter when he failed to stop and consider what kind of situation he was in. He automatically assumed that he was still in a social situation, one in which he could threaten, negotiate, and communicate his way to a satisfactory resolution. He wanted to establish that he was mad. He wanted to make the man capitulate. *"You're going to listen to me. You're going to fix my car."* He didn't consider the possibility that the man inside was operating in an entirely different world—that he was facing life in prison, that Alex was an impediment to his escape, and that he was willing to kill to solve his immediate problem.

To most people, there would be few things in this world more intimidating than a champion martial artist, boxing gloves still on, screaming and banging on the driver's-side window. But here's the problem with intimidation: it's like juggling thirteen double-edged swords and playing with fire at the same time. Intimidation—those strutting, peacocking displays that we associate with social aggression—is a dare. It's a way of saying *I'm about to hurt you.* And, *Go ahead, try to*

---

* "Fender-bender hit-run turns fatal in S.F. / Kickbox champ chases down driver, winds up shot to death," SFGate.com, August 2, 2003, www.sfgate .com/news/article/Fender-bender-hit-run-turns-fatal-in-S-F-2598674.php.

hurt me first — see what happens. Sometimes, your adversary receives the message you're trying to communicate and backs down. But sometimes, he calls your bluff. Sometimes, he's on the same page as you are, and he's going to engage you in a round of social aggression. But sometimes, he'll be like the man who shot Alex — someone who doesn't give a damn about your rules.

Intimidation can get you killed. It's a sucker's game.

All Alex needed to do to avert a deadly conflict was stay put. All he needed to do to resolve the legal issues with the car was get the man's license plate number, which he could have done from his parking lot. Sadly, Alex was so enraged that he never paused to ask himself if provoking a confrontation would be worth it. He had car insurance! Scraped cars get repaired all the time! If he took a moment to step back from the immediate situation — to imagine the consequences from three days in the future of provoking a confrontation with a total stranger who was willing to flee the scene of an accident at high speed — I can guarantee you that chasing the driver down wouldn't have been worth it to Alex.

This is not the easiest thing in the world to do. Choking down rage in favor of reason can take what feels like superhuman strength. The most reliable way to make it easier is to meditate and visualize consequences ahead of time so that, in the heat of the moment, you're relying on the decision-making skills you've honed through sober practice rather than raw instinct. Whether the right course of action is de-escalating, or fighting for your life, your reactions need to be automatic — but they also need to be correct.

So how do we get it right? How do we know when we're in

a confrontation that requires avoidance and social reasoning, and when we're in a confrontation in which social reasoning goes out the window and calls for immediate action?

Avoiding the worst-case scenario—walking away from an unnecessary fight, or acting in time to save your life in an unavoidable fight—often means making effective snap judgments. Here's the simple litmus test I use: if there's communication going on—if the other person is talking to you, even if it's aggressively or insultingly—you're still in social aggression mode, which means you should run away, or use your social skills to negotiate your way out of the confrontation. If there's no communication, or the other person is already in the process of taking physical action, and there's no available exit, the situation is asocial. You're facing imminent grievous bodily harm and your only option at that point is to fight back.

Think of it like this: If you find yourself asking, "Should I hit him?" the answer is probably *No.*

The only reason you are even asking is because something deep down inside of you has recognized that, from a social and moral point of view, there's something iffy about responding to the situation with violence. It's the little angel of conscience on your shoulder, whispering in your ear.

And if the answer is *No,* sometimes that means backing down. Sometimes that will challenge your ego, and it might mean accepting some degree of humiliation. You might be called a coward. But you'll be alive, and free. Unless you would feel comfortable *and justified* emptying a firearm into the threat in front you—an action that would almost certainly result in their death—it's time to walk away.

JUST GET TO THE REST OF YOUR DAY

Walking away can be *hard*. I know. On my worst days, it's a struggle to be patient and let the stupid stuff slide, especially when the other guy has justified my anger. My ego is no help in these situations, either. What if I look weak? Am I really going to let him "win"?

My answer is, yes, absolutely. Anything that gets me on to the rest of my day and the rest of my life is the real victory. In life-or-death moments, this means hurting people. But in the realm of social aggression, you should always try to avoid the avoidable.

When you're seriously provoked by a jerk, part of you may want to face him down with your best icy stare (this is certainly how my bouncer friend Mike felt). Part of you may want to tell him just where he can stuff it, and then, if he doesn't get the message, lay him out on the sidewalk. That'll show him. And make a hell of a story to tell your friends, to boot. At its core, this behavior is an impulse that is instinctive to the human species. It's about dominance and status and placement in the social hierarchy. It's textbook social aggression. Since most of us have evolved into sane, socialized people, however, we have managed to contain the impulse to the realm of fantasy.

Every man at some point in his life, for instance, has lain awake at night imagining what it would be like to deliver some karmic retribution, or take down an intruder, or put a bully in his place, or disarm an active shooter. We plan it out. We envision an entire scenario. We create context and backstory. We game out, in exquisite detail, exactly what the villains are going to do and what we are going to do in response. There is blood and breaking bones and few words, but none of it is real. Not that our bodies can tell the difference. If you examined us in that moment, you'd find that our hearts are beating faster, our adrenaline is spiked, we're so engrossed in the scene playing out in our heads that we have lost all sense of time and place.

This coping mechanism for our innate, aggressive impulses—particularly when we feel we've been wronged—is so universal that you can find it reflected in our entertainment, which is rife with this kind of fantastical violence. Jason Bourne, John McClane, even so-called wimps like Marty McFly and Daniel LaRusso, these are the hero archetypes constructed for our entertainment, from our natural tendencies. Saving hostages, fighting back against bullies, protecting the homestead, defending against evil, evening the score, these are the situations our heroes find themselves in, because these are the ways, historically, that we have felt threatened and victimized. And so, these are the types of outlandish, zero-sum scenarios we have bouncing around in our imaginations when we've been provoked and we're, as Howard Beale shouted into the camera in the great 1976 film *Network*, "mad as hell and...not going to take this anymore." We are Malcolm X at the window. Kevin McCallister at the top of the stairs. Chris Kyle at the long gun.

But I think we all know those fantasies are not how reality tends to work out.

You risk getting stabbed or shot to death, getting knocked down and brained on the concrete. At the very least, you're probably not getting out of your situation without getting hurt yourself. And then there are the legal consequences.

Are you getting sued for medical expenses or charged with assault? Are you going to prison for manslaughter?

And for what?

It's so much easier to let it go whenever and wherever you can, to claim your moral victory, and to just get to the rest of your day. Be man or woman enough to be called a coward, and walk away whenever you have the chance.

I've walked away from more situations than I can count where no one present would have objected if I'd laid some jerk out. I've walked away while dodging ego-withering epithets and slurs, to the accompaniment of the loud and obvious sound of my social standing being taken down a notch and my position as invincible father being called into question.

In 2006, I was on the cover of *Black Belt* magazine. The weekend after my issue came out, I had a training seminar scheduled in San Diego. My seminars start early, so I took my son Conner, who was not even ten years old at the time, to hang out with my brother, who was working with a company that was testing amazing, next-generation speed boats that SEAL teams were looking to use. Conner was going to spend the day with his uncle riding around in cool boats, I was going to run my seminar, and then we were all going out to dinner later that night. When Conner got in the car he was proudly carrying my issue of *Black Belt*. It was shaping up to be a really cool day.

Not long into our drive from North County down to the bay where my brother was, we came to the top of a blind hill. It was a tricky juncture in a hilly, residential area, and when I came up the hill I couldn't see over its crest; I could only see so much of the road to my left, where I was headed. To the right, the hill was still going up, so downhill oncoming traffic was effectively in my blind spot. Being so early and with the roads quiet, I didn't think much about making the left turn down the hill. But then, just as I made it into the middle of the intersection, a car came screaming down the hill from our right, swerved around us, leaned on the horn, and then, despite having another lane to work with, swerved back in front of us and stayed there for a minute just to make his point.

At the stoplight at the bottom of the hill, Conner and I rolled to a stop and pulled up next to the maniac who'd just come at us like a bat out of hell. In the moment I didn't think anything of it, I just laughed it off. It was a beautiful morning, Conner and I had our windows down, if a honked horn was the worst thing that happened to us that day, we should be so lucky. Then the guy looked over and opened his mouth.

"I should just kick your ass." It had been a good twenty years since I'd trained to be a legally sanctioned killing machine, but aside from some gray hair, I still looked the part. I'm a big dude, I'm in really good shape, I have a couple tattoos on my arm. Guys who look like me are generally not the ones you randomly threaten with physical violence. But I couldn't take the bait.

"Oh, sorry man," I said, "I didn't mean to get in your way. I didn't see you."

"Yeah, yeah, whatever," he said. My apology didn't seem to satisfy him. I could tell he was looking for a fight. "Look at you with your tattoo and your muscles. You think you can fight. You can't fight. I'd kick your ass right now."

He was doing everything he could to egg me on, just hoping to show me up in front of my son. Conner was paying full attention. He was looking at the guy next to us, then looking back at me. And the whole time he's holding the issue of *Black Belt* with me on the cover.

"Hey, I'm really sorry you feel that way. Again, I apologize. I hope you have a nice day."

Finally, the light turned green, the guy cursed at me one last time for good measure, and then sped off. I took my foot off the brake and continued at our normal speed. Conner was very confused.

"But Dad, why didn't you get out? Why didn't you kick his butt? He was nothing. You could've killed him!" he said, in the way young boys use the word "kill" without fully understanding what it means.

Of course, Conner was right. With my skillset and my physical advantage, there was a very good chance I would win a confrontation against that man, all things being equal. But that's just it: we didn't know if they were equal. We didn't know if he was carrying a weapon. We didn't know how unstable he was. What if he decided to use his car as a weapon and crash into us? I explained all of this to Conner but he still didn't quite understand.

"You should have said something, Dad. Don't let him talk to you like that. You're *this guy!*" he said, pointing to the cover of the magazine.

"Exactly," I said, "I'm that guy, not the guy who gets into fights in the middle of the street. I hope you remember that."

I'm not going to lie. I wanted to beat the living crap out of that guy. It would have been so gratifying—as a man, a father, and a role model—to shove all those words right back down that guy's throat and prove my son right, that nobody can talk to his dad like that. But that was the ego talking. That was the immature guy with the John McClane fantasies.

I'm not that guy. I couldn't be. I had my young son to con-sider. What if I got stabbed or shot? What if I "won" our con-frontation and the other guy got grievously injured and I got arrested? I'd have to spend the day in jail (at least), make bail, maybe get charged, almost definitely get sued, pay a law-yer, and on and on. What would happen to Conner? What would happen to my business, to my reputation in the com-munity, to my lifestyle? And for what: because some guy was having a bad morning and made fun of me? It wasn't worth it, and unless it involved saving my life or the life of my son, it never would be. So I chose to de-escalate and drive away.

REAL VIOLENCE IS UNPREDICTABLE

Here's another reason to walk away whenever possible: when you escalate a situation into the realm of serious physical harm, no one—and that emphatically includes you—can predict the outcome. You're risking your own life, like Alex did—and you're also risking delivering far more harm than you intended. Those risks are worth taking when your life is indisputably on the line—in those scenarios there is no such thing as too much harm—but they're not worth taking for any other reason.

Read the news, and you'll find stories like that all the time, stories of unnecessary escalation gone horribly wrong. Maybe you read about one of those incidents that took place at a youth hockey practice in Massachusetts.* The cops from

---

* "Father in Killing at Hockey Rink Is Given Sentence of 6 to 10 Years," *New York Times,* January 26, 2002, www.nytimes.com/2002/01/26/us/father-in-killing-at-hockey-rink-is-given-sentence-of-6-to-10-years.html.

the town where the incident occurred attended one of my training seminars and told me what has come to be a very familiar-sounding story.

A father was attending a non-contact scrimmage in which his young son was playing. The man supervising and coaching the scrimmage was known for being rough with the kids and letting things get more physical than was safe or necessary. The father was a truck driver and a big man—6'5", maybe 300 pounds—with a quick temper. The coach was much smaller but towered over most of the kids. At one point during the scrimmage, the hockey dad's son took an elbow to the face from another player.

"Hey! You better stop them from doing that!" the father yelled.

The coach looked over at the father and yelled back, "That's hockey!" Effectively challenging his masculinity. The father stormed down to the ice and confronted the couch. After an initial exchange that got broken up, things got heated again and the two came back together. That's when things got ugly in a hurry. After a few seconds, both men were brawling on the thinly matted concrete floor just off the ice. They tumbled to the ground. The dad got on top of the coach, pinned him down by the shirt, and punched him in the head repeatedly.

The father didn't realize it, but every time he punched the coach, he was basically slamming the back of his head into a rock-hard surface. Suddenly there was blood—and then silence. He had ruptured an artery in the coach's neck. Inadvertently, the dad had killed the coach right in front of his son and the rest of the team—which included the coach's three sons who were also playing. All four boys were under the age of fourteen. Ego, frustration, bad behavior, and then ultimately a poor understanding of physics and anatomy ended two lives: one man was buried, and the other was incarcerated.

Neither man woke up that morning spoiling for a fight. According to the cops at my training seminar, neither even wanted to fight in the moment when things got heated. But once they'd crossed each other's physical plane—an act of which they were both guilty—all bets were off and that's when everything went horribly wrong.

WHO SAYS WE'RE USING *YOUR* RULES?

One of my clients is married to a man who is originally from the French island of Corsica in the Mediterranean Sea. They met in the United States, but they held their wedding back in his small hometown. It's not easy to get to Corsica, and from the time Napoleon was born there everyone has been trying to get *out* of Corsica. It was a smaller wedding. Mostly family and close friends.

My client's father was a prominent Washington, DC, lawyer—tall, influential with politicians, and very accus-tomed to getting his way.

On the first morning in Corsica, he decided to go across the street to a little market to pick up a few things. He browsed the shop's shelves, struggled through the language barrier as he paid, and then on his way back to the hotel, he crossed the street without waiting for the light to change.

As he stepped out into the street, a car sped around the corner and nearly hit him as it approached a red light just up the road. This enraged my client's father, and he was going to let the driver know about it. He started yelling and slapping his hand against the side of the car, making a total scene. The driver opened the door and got out. He was dressed immaculately, like a Wall Street executive. He didn't say a word. He walked straight up to her father, balled up his fist, and smashed him on the tip of his nose with a hammer punch—using the pinky end of his fist—knocking him to the ground. As her father hit the pavement, most of his teeth got knocked out. He couldn't believe it. There he was, a distinguished American attorney *and* the father of the bride, holding on to a fistful of his teeth, like so many Chiclets.

Two policemen who happened to be nearby ran up. "Oh, thank goodness," he thought. "The cops are here." He pointed at the driver accusingly, but the cops wouldn't stop yelling at *him*. The father didn't speak French, so he couldn't understand what they were saying, but later he found out they were saying they had seen everything, and that *he* was the person who made the mistake. They said he was lucky to be alive.

Obviously, my client's father had completely misread the situation. He didn't think of the cultural differences in play. He was accustomed to United States law and custom, where he would have been viewed as the victim of assault. He was used to a world where the pedestrian always has the right-of-way and is entitled to express himself at the driver. In Corsica, the cops weren't sympathetic to this worldview—they saw him as the instigator. He just *assumed* everybody was operating under the same social contract.

You don't have to be in a foreign country to find yourself in a similar situation. When you're interacting with someone you don't know, you simply cannot take it for granted that they share your assumptions about what is and isn't allowed, about what will and will not lead to violence. You can't assume that others are reluctant to use violence against you or that they view escalation as something to be avoided. Until you know that person, they're foreign to *you*.

That's why, wherever possible, the smart play is politeness, accommodation, and de-escalation. Unfortunately, we don't learn that from movies, because polite, de-escalating accommodation doesn't feel very satisfying when we're especially aggrieved. Interestingly, criminals often understand that better than law-abiding citizens like my client's father. As the author Robert E. Howard wrote, "civilized men are more discourteous than savages because they know they can be impolite without having their skulls split, as a general thing."* It's a phenomenon I first learned about from Charles Poliquin, the renowned strength coach.

Charles Poliquin travels all over the world to train elite athletes and law enforcement officers. When he gets to a new town, he always asks one of the cops he's going to be working with, "Where do most of the ex-felons and criminals work out?" It's a question that catches most people by surprise. They wonder why on earth anyone would want to know that. But Poliquin wants to know because that's the gym where he wants to work out, too.

Why there? Because, as he explains, "the people tend to be far more polite and allow each other to work out without interfering or getting in the way."

The assumption built into Poliquin's statement is that the

---

* The line appears in Howard's 1933 story, "The Tower of the Elephant." Howard is most famous for creating the character Conan the Barbarian.

people from "polite society" who work out at nicer gyms are *not* so polite. (Anyone who's had a run-in with the kind of jerk who acts like the treadmill is his personal property or that the squat rack is a great place to take a phone call is probably nodding their head right now.) What Poliquin understands is that criminals and felons come from a world defined by an entirely different social contract than yours or mine—a world where you can't afford to disrespect each other without the risk of real violence. What this means for them, if they want to have any peace in their lives, is that in an environment like a gym, it's better to be polite and understanding.

In my own life, I generally operate as if I'm at the run-down gym, not the nicely-polished fitness chain. That's how you should operate, too. If I'm talking to someone I don't already know personally—a foreigner to me—I assume two things: 1) we don't live by the same social contract, and 2) I'm six seconds away from them unleashing a shooting spree. That doesn't mean I'm jumpy and paranoid. It means I'm as kind and considerate as possible. If every stranger lived by a different set of rules (at best) or was just looking for a reason to start firing (at worst) how would you interact with them? You'd be polite and accommodating, too.

Criminals don't need to be taught this lesson, or if they did, they only had to learn it once. The rest of us, though, are prone to making the bad assumption that the other guy in any given conflict is operating under the very same rules we're taking for granted. Maybe the contract you imagine says, "You're allowed to call each other 'asshole.' You're allowed to get in each other's faces. A honk is just another way to send a message to another driver and not an unforgivable assault on someone's honor. And if anyone breaks the contract, you can always sue—so don't worry." This is why the jerk on the next treadmill over at your Gold's Gym is such a jerk—he's not expecting any serious consequences.

But what do you do when you're up against someone who does not live by the same social contract? What if he couldn't care less about your rules? What if he has rules of his own? What if he has no rules at all? If that's possible, *why would you take the chance of provoking him?*

If provocation is the lifeblood of social aggression, then the absence of prevention is the lifeblood of asocial violence. Like lightning to metal, mold to darkness, and mushrooms to moisture, asocial violence thrives on the unaware, the unprepared, and the absentminded. The rest of this chapter is dedicated to prevention, to making your environment less hospitable to the probing, indiscriminate nature of asocial violence.

DOING NOTHING IS DOING EVERYTHING WRONG

Rick (not his real name) is a highly successful entrepreneur. He has founded multiple companies. His net worth was in the hundreds of millions by the time he was thirty. After cashing out of his businesses, he decided to retire early. He commissioned his dream home to be built in a newly developed gated community in Naples, Florida. He and his wife were heavily involved in the design process, custom building the interior—it was a labor of love.

Originally the home was scheduled to be move-in-ready by their anniversary. It wasn't planned that way; it was just the luck of the calendar, one of those bits of serendipity that happens when things are going your way. As is usually the case with construction—and everything in the state of Florida—major delays in the months leading up to their anniversary made move-in on the day impossible. They'd gotten close to making the house livable, but there were still major things left to do. The marble floor on the first floor still needed to be installed. Some of the door hardware hadn't come in yet. There was some key HVAC and wiring work to do still.

As an entrepreneur, Rick was accustomed to improvising, so the delays didn't bother him as much as they did his wife. To soothe her irritation, he decided to plan a special anniversary surprise for her. He instructed the builders to put all non-essential work aside and complete the master bedroom suite, from the electrical wiring to the finishes. Rick wanted their room to look like someone took a suite from the Ritz-Carlton and dropped it into the middle of a full home remodel. He hired a chef and a full waitstaff for the evening and organized a candlelight dinner to be set up in the room.

The night went off without a hitch. Rick and his wife celebrated their anniversary with a five-star meal in the bedroom suite where they hoped to spend the rest of their lives together. After the meal, the waitstaff cleaned up, sealed the plastic over the lockless front door, and left Rick and his wife to a warm bath and a soft bed. It was a perfect anniversary.

Then, around two-thirty a.m., everything went sour. Rick's wife woke to the sound of the plastic over the front door and footsteps on the subfloor downstairs. Someone was in the house. Rick put on some clothes to go investigate, but before he could even make it out of their bedroom, the door was kicked down and five masked men with shotguns barged in, yelling at them in Spanish.

Rick froze. He had no idea what to do. He instinctively put his hands up, but that didn't seem to stop them. One of the men slammed the butt of his shotgun into Rick's forehead, knocking him down. The others grabbed him, tied him up, yelling at him the whole time. But Rick couldn't understand — he didn't speak Spanish.

This only seemed to piss off the men more. Two of them went over to the bed — the soft, warm, safe place where Rick and his wife had just celebrated a wonderful marriage and a bright future — and grabbed Rick's wife. They gagged her and tied her hands with duct tape. Then they took turns sexually assaulting her as Rick watched in horror. Finally, if that weren't enough, they hit Rick over and over and over again, beating him nearly to death, before leaving. There was no theft. Nothing was taken. After wriggling out of their bindings, Rick and his wife called 911.

The violent, horrifying attack made no sense. The Naples police department couldn't figure it out. They interviewed Rick and his wife multiple times, but found no indications pointing to any potential suspects. Rick had no enemies that he knew of — not even a lawsuit against him or one of his companies. He and his wife both had squeaky-clean records. They never bought drugs or associated with criminals. They were model citizens.

Then, three weeks after the attack, a DEA representative contacted the police station and the mystery came to an utterly unsatisfying conclusion. It turns out the whole incident was a case of mistaken identity — a horrible fluke, a banal error of unspeakable evil. The masked men were part of a drug cartel who had been ripped off by a drug dealer who happened to live in a mansion that looked similar to the façade of Rick's new home. The masked men were sent to deliver a message. Unfortunately for Rick and his wife, that message was meant for the house four doors down. When Rick froze in the bedroom, the drug dealers just assumed he was scared shitless. They had no idea he couldn't understand them.

I spend my career teaching people the tools they can use to protect themselves against life-or-death violence. But nothing I teach would have equipped Rick with the tools to defeat five armed men. When I eventually did meet Rick, that's precisely what I told him—and not just to make him feel better. I told him there was nothing he could have done to avoid the horrific things that occurred once the bedroom door was knocked down. That's how life goes. Past a certain point, there is often little that we can do. The key, then, is to find the point before that point, the place where specific changes might change the course of your life for the better.

There were steps Rick could have taken to stop this event *before* it happened. I want to think through those steps, because none of them involved the execution of violence. Unlike many of the cases I have discussed so far in this book, and will discuss in the chapters to come, this is one where violence was *not* the answer, where violence—even if Rick knew what to do—was a losing proposition because some asocial situations are simply impossible to escape once you're in them. Instead, this is a story where the only answer may have been an ounce or two of prevention.

Rick made several poor decisions that night. I want to

stress that those decisions do not in any way make him responsible for what happened—the responsibility falls on the criminals alone. There's no "blaming the victims" here, because there's no question of where the blame lies. But we can still learn from those mistakes to protect ourselves from those who would do us harm.

First, Rick chose to spend the night in an unfinished mansion; the security system wasn't up and running, and he didn't have any doors to lock. Because the community was gated, he assumed it was safe. It wasn't safe—not from drug dealers, as we found out, but also not safe from thieves who might want to steal his appliances or rip out the copper wiring going into the walls. An intruder could have very easily entered the open bottom floor with nonviolent intent, but ended up doing something different.

Second, he didn't bring his dog to deter any home invaders. And finally, there were no outdoor lights or motion detectors on around the house, meaning that the attackers could approach, enter, and exit unseen. If the drug dealers found a well-lit home with locked doors, a security system, and a dog—they might have just walked away and looked for another opportunity.

These aren't what-ifs, either. The police eventually caught two of the five masked men, who later confessed to the break-in. They said they were surprised there was no security in the house. They also said they would have waited for another opportunity to target their victim at a different location if they had heard or seen a dog. For want of a nail—or in this case, a door, or a dog—Rick's entire life turned out differently than it should have.

This is an extreme story. Most of us aren't hanging out in

unlocked mansions at night. More to the point, the specifics of any situation of real-world violence matter far less than the big principles that underpin them. If all you take from Rick's story is "don't hang out in an unlocked mansion," you're missing the big picture: Rick had lived a blessed life up to that point. He was well-liked, and he had never experienced violence before. Sadly, his good fortune led him to let his guard down. It led him to be unprepared when violence finally found him.

Fortunately, there are preventive measures we can take to minimize the chances of violence like this ever entering our lives — little things that, cumulatively, can make a big difference to our safety. Here are a few more.

HEADPHONES AND SMARTPHONES

If there is one common thread to all the surveillance videos of male-on-female attacks that I have studied over the years, it is the presence of headphones on the woman's head. When you wear headphones, you lose environmental awareness. When you take away your sense of hearing, you've handicapped yourself before an assailant even enters the picture. Without your sense of hearing, you're a prime target for mugging, sexual assault, and any other crime that relies on the element of surprise.

I know we all love listening to music and podcasts and audiobooks. But if you're alone in an urban environment, especially an unfamiliar one, I recommend you keep your ears unobstructed. You're trading a few minutes of entertainment for hundreds of thousands of years of evolutionary advantages bestowed on you by your ears and eyes.

Ironically, among those of us who play by normal social rules, headphones have always felt like a kind of protection. They're a clear signal that we don't want to be bothered. Among those who follow the rules, they block out conversations and unwanted advances. But by wearing headphones, you're *attracting* the type of people you most want to avoid: those who do not respect normal social rules. What works in a social environment can be deadly in an asocial environment—and the two types of atmospheres can flip within seconds.

Even without wearing headphones, staring at your phone can also be dangerous. I saw surveillance video of a bus ride in Seattle that brought this notion into stark relief. It was a normal, downtown bus filled with passengers from every walk of life. All of them were immersed in their phones. They weren't looking at each other. They weren't interacting. They weren't aware of their surroundings. Then, a criminal starts walking down the aisle of the bus with a loaded weapon (a .45 caliber pistol) pointing it in people's faces and taking their phones, jewelry, and wallets. He goes from person to person without anyone noticing. It's all happening in plain sight, but to those just rows in front of him, he might as well have been invisible. People were so disconnected from their environment that he was able to catch everyone off guard. And after each person's items were taken, they were too shaken to say anything or warn anyone else.

Toward the end of the video clip, one guy on the bus finally becomes aware of what's happening. He redirects the firearm and starts pushing toward the guy, which is good. But in his other hand, he's holding his iPhone. Instead of using the phone as an improvised weapon, or at the very least dropping it so he has the full use of both of his hands, he tries to tuck it away into his pocket. Even when faced with life-or-death situations, our first thought is to protect our mobile devices before fighting for our lives. A poor, unthinking modern man is staring down a .45 caliber bullet and he's worried about cracking his screen.

Luckily, the rest of the passengers on the bus were able to help out and knock the robber to the ground. The man was arrested and nobody got hurt, but they were lucky. I don't want my clients to have to rely on luck. I want them to be trained, aware, and prepared. It all begins with a basic awareness of your surroundings—the simplest and easiest thing you can do to protect yourself.

SECLUSION AT NIGHT

Nicole duFresne was an actress and playwright. One night, she went out with her boyfriend and another couple to a nightclub on the Lower East Side of Manhattan. When they left the club, they decided to walk home instead of taking a cab. They only lived four blocks away, but that was four too many. A few strides beyond the exit to the club, they were confronted by a group of teenagers who'd been cruising around all night harassing people and attempting to mug them. The ringleader, a nineteen-year-old man named Rudy Fleming, pistol-whipped Nicole's fiancé over the eye, knocking him to the ground. He then snatched her friend's purse and tossed it to two of his female partners — one of whom was only fourteen years old at the time — then demanded that everyone in the group hand over their money.

They all complied, except for Nicole, who was enraged by Fleming's treatment of her fiancé. She got right up in his face: "What are you going to do, you going to shoot us? Is that what you wanted?!" He pushed her away but she came right back at him, repeating her same question: "What are you going to do, shoot us?!" Fleming paused for a moment, and then pulled the trigger, firing a single shot into Nicole's chest. She fell back and bled to death in her fiancé's arms as the teenage muggers ran.[*]

This happened in the early morning hours, around three a.m. Nicole and her friends could have easily taken a cab, but they didn't. It might seem silly to take a cab only four blocks, but in the middle of the night, it's not so silly. If you've read this far, you've probably also recognized how Nicole escalated a situation that didn't need to be escalated — her social aggression turned the scenario asocial — but that's beside the point. The first mistake she made was walking home.[†] The second was thinking that material possessions are ever worth your life.

Sure, taxis and valet parking services cost a bit of money. But they cost next to nothing compared to the cost of going

---

[*] "Woman's Defiance Led Mugger to Kill Her, Accomplice Testifies," *New York Times*, October 5, 2006, www.nytimes.com/2006/10/05/nyregion/05kill.html.

[†] The Lower East Side is a much different place now than it was when Nicole and her friends were attacked — that's why you must always be aware of your specific surroundings. You never know when your immediate environment can change around you.

out for the night — think of them as a small insurance policy on your night out, one that keeps you in safe spaces and minimizes the chances of violence finding you. I think your physical safety is worth a cab fare or a parking fee.

Most people overlook this kind of insurance not because they can't afford it, but because they underestimate the value of preventive measures against black swan events like antisocial violence. That's the nature of black swan events, after all — they're relatively cheap to hedge against, but they're so unlikely that most people don't bother to hedge at all. And that's devastating, because, as unlikely as being the victim of antisocial violence may be, it can have life-changing consequences in the rare event that it does come to pass. Protecting yourself — in this case, with a cab or a valet service — isn't a Cadillac plan reserved for the wealthy. It's an insurance policy for everyone.

DO YOUR HABITS MAKE YOU A TARGET?

Greg (not his real name) was a senior official in a maximum-security prison who was very good at his job. He maintained his authority and kept order, like every corrections officer should, but he also kept his ear to the ground, gathering intelligence from prisoners he spoke with on an almost daily basis. Getting the inside scoop on things going down in the yard so you can interdict before they happen is a big part of keeping order.

Greg had a strong relationship with one prisoner in particular, whom I'll call Randy. The men were by no means friends — their interactions were very formal — but there was enough respect there that each knew the other could help keep them more informed. Each man's survival depended not just on his ability to effectively use violence when called upon, but also to never be caught unaware.

One day, Greg was doing his normal rounds and checked in with Randy. They asked each other questions that neither one could answer fully, but were important for maintaining the open line of communication. When the conversation started to trail off, Randy changed the subject and got serious.

"Listen man, you've got to change up how you carry your equipment."

"What are you talking about?"

"You're wearing your keys on your right side. And the way you're walking—I could spear you in the neck."

"What did you just say to me?" Greg said. He wasn't sure if Randy was needling him or threatening him. Turns out it was neither: he was warning him.

"You're walking too close to the cages. I could spear you and then take your keys. Look, it's not me you have to worry about. It's everyone else."

"Don't worry about me, inmate. I can handle myself." As a prison guard, you can never appear to be weak. Randy continued anyway.

"I know for a fact that it takes you twenty-nine steps from the stairs to get to my cell. I know when you approach me, there's a specific part of your neck and torso exposed. Believe me—there are guys in here who are planning for that day when you come by and get distracted and they can get a shot at you."

"What are you trying to tell me here, brother?" Randy's

words were getting very specific. It felt to Greg like he was trying to subtly communicate some directly actionable piece of information.

"You need to make some changes to throw them off balance. I'm tellin' you, if you don't, someone's gonna take you out, grab your keys, let themselves out, let everyone else out, and start a riot. You'll be dead. And this place will be a madhouse."

When the officers did a cell check on Randy's block later that month, they found a cache of weapons—including sharpened sticks—spread around a number of cells, many of which housed inmates whom Greg stopped to talk with on a regular basis. They also found chalked outlines on the walls behind beds that matched the shape and height of various guards, including Greg. There were scrape marks concentrated in clusters at various spots inside the outlines: prisoners had been practicing exactly where to strike to cause a serious injury. Randy hadn't been speaking in hypotheticals—Greg had been one slip away from a brutal death.

Any job, no matter how dangerous it appears from the outside, can become boring or monotonous after a while. Corrections is no exception. Greg had gotten lost in the routine of his daily duties and the casual nature of his interactions with prisoners. He was getting complacent and predictable with his approach to his work. Randy gave him an important, timely, and potentially life-saving reminder: *"You're doing things that make you a target."*

Predictability, routine, complacency, obliviousness.

These are characteristics that compose the ideal target

for acts of asocial violence. Taking the same route to and from work makes the journey routine and puts it on autopilot. Who hasn't left their house and arrived at the subway entrance or the front door of the office and had no recollection of how they got there? How many of us run to the store with our earbuds in and our eyes on our Twitter feeds? Each of those behaviors is just another ring on the target you may be painting on your back without knowing it.

They are what turn someone into a not-so-random victim of random acts of violence like the knockout game. They contributed to making Sara a target for her assaulter instead of any other young woman with a first-floor dorm room. She and her roommate had slipped into a comfortable routine. They regularly left the window unlocked. Her roommate consistently stayed over at her boyfriend's place on certain nights. And the serial rapist who had been terrorizing campuses for years had catalogued that information just like the Black Guerilla Family members did with the CERT team's new gear, and the men in Randy's cellblock did with Greg's work habits.

What behaviors do you engage in consistently or automatically that might make *you* a target? Do you always have your headphones on? Do you sleep with the window open? Do you take money out of the ATM at the same time and location each week? These habits make you vulnerable to opportunistic predators. Fortunately, they are easy to correct, and the changes may very well save your life.

But don't thank me. Thank Randy, the violent criminal doing life in a maximum-security prison. By looking out for Greg, he ended up looking out for you, too.

MAN'S BEST FRIEND

People often ask me, "What's the best security system for my home?" Without hesitation, I tell them to get a dog. If you don't want to take my word for it, listen to the thousands of law enforcement officers who will happily tell you that nothing deters criminals like a dog. We're not talking about a trained, purebred, $40,000 German Shepherd or Belgian Malinois here, either.* I'm not even talking about an attack dog. I'm talking about anything that barks. That bark is nature's burglar alarm. When your dog starts barking out of nowhere, in the middle of the night, at an unusual volume or frequency, it's telling you that someone or something strange just entered their sensory zone.

What makes a dog so advantageous from a security perspective is that it can't be shut down, disabled, or worked around like an alarm. A criminal can't prevent a dog from issuing its warning because it usually senses the criminal before the criminal even knows it's there. Sure, a burglar can try to shut a dog up by killing it or corralling it in some other way. But if they shoot it, they've fired their weapon and lost the element of surprise. And if they try to corral it against its will, you can be sure the dog is going to make a whole bunch of other noise. No matter what, it's nearly impossible to prevent a dog from warning its owner about strangers in their midst.

---

* That said, if you have the money and love large, loyal, long-haired dogs, you could do worse than the Shepherd or the Malinois. Those are the breeds American Special Operations Forces train to go into battle with them. They are exceptional protectors.

Criminals are generally risk-averse enough that a barking dog is a sufficient deterrent. Like Rick's attackers, they'd rather take a softer target. But even if that doesn't happen, a dog's warning signal gives its owner extra time to react. Maybe it's only fifteen or thirty seconds—but that can make all the difference in the world when your life's on the line.

Dogs are like taxis: they aren't free, and lots of people would rather forgo the expense (and, in the case of a dog, the responsibility), but they're still one of the best and cheapest insurance policies you can buy against life-altering violence. They're four-legged security blankets, whether on the sofa at home or on a leash walking with you to the store.

MAKE YOURSELF A DIFFICULT TARGET

I cannot emphasize enough how important it is to remember that real-life violence isn't a competition. Predators aren't looking for a challenge. If you give them enough hoops to jump through, more often than not they're going to pick someone else. They're looking for the easiest victim—the lowest-hanging fruit. It's like that old joke about the two hikers in the forest who come across a hungry bear. One of them stops to put on his running shoes. The other tells him not to bother, since there's no way a person can outrun a bear. His hiking partner says, "I don't have to outrun the bear. I only have to outrun you." Be the hiker in the running shoes.

But what does a difficult target look like? A difficult target is aware of his or her surroundings. A difficult target never takes away one of his or her sensory systems in public: he or she never voluntarily limits the senses of sight, sound, smell, taste, or touch. Anything that hampers your senses makes you more attractive to a predator.

At home, a difficult target takes basic precautions. Difficult targets lock their doors. They keep their windows shut and locked at night. They own security systems, they keep exterior lights on to thwart home invaders, and they keep at least one light on inside the house. Difficult targets own dogs.

Lastly, a difficult target walks and moves with confidence — the confidence that comes from knowing that he or she, in the last resort, can deploy the tool of violence when it's necessary. That confidence shows in your body language and on your face — it's a constant and silent deterrent. It says, *pick on somebody else.*

As we're about to explore in detail, you don't have to be a jiujitsu master or a physical specimen to inflict injury. You don't have to be a paranoid "prepper" or an expert tactician. Here is all you need: the confidence to de-escalate conflict whenever possible, the confidence that comes from taking basic precautions in your life, and the confidence that comes from knowing you can use the tool of violence as a last resort.

It's the last one that we're going to dive into now — those moments when you cannot de-escalate, those moments when your precautions can't save you, those moments when you have no choice but to fight for your life. What do you do when you can't walk or run away? How do you respond effectively when you find yourself trapped? If you're forced to use the tool of violence, how can you turn the odds in your favor? As we'll see in Part 2, it begins and ends with understanding the principles that set the foundation for how *to use* violence.

PART 2

HOW TO THINK ABOUT *USING* VIOLENCE

CHAPTER SIX

THE BEST TARGET IS THE ONE YOU CAN GET

While we stop to think, we often miss our opportunity.
— *Publilius Syrus*

Bonnie (not her real name) was one of the 70 percent. By the time she showed up at one of my two-day live training seminars, it was too late to prevent her from becoming victimized by frightening violence. It had already happened. She had been violently assaulted and become a statistic. Her experiences made it more difficult for her to learn and digest the material I was throwing at her and the other class members because it dredged up fearful memories of the attack she was still struggling to overcome. It was so hard, in fact, she needed to come back and go through the seminar a second time.

Between the two sessions, Bonnie was diagnosed with PTSD, got a concealed-carry permit, bought a gun for protection, and was given a therapy dog to help her manage the anxiety of daily living. It seemed to help. The physical elements of training were easier for her to grasp and execute the second time around. Still, she was nervous about applying in the real world the principles I was trying to teach her. Because she had been attacked, attacking seemed unnatural (she had absorbed what I would call a victim's mindset) and the whole concept of using violence felt immoral and uncomfortable.

After the last session on the second day, I pulled Bonnie aside and had a conversation with her that was equal parts "heart to heart" and "come to Jesus." I reminded Bonnie that she was a good person, that she hadn't deserved what happened to her, and that every principle I taught was designed only to be used to save her own life. More important, I told her that she had found herself trapped in a violent situation because, for whatever reason, her assailant had identified her as a target. What she needed to understand now was that those reasons might become more pronounced if they weren't addressed. And if she were to ever find herself in another encounter, she had to be able to turn the tables and identify *him* (or *her*) as a target if she wanted to survive.

A few months later, Bonnie was at the Home Depot near her home picking up some gardening supplies. She was in the parking lot, preparing to load her purchases into the trunk of her car. Bags of potting soil, flats of begonias, stakes for the tomato plants she was going to grow. Normal stuff. She had them on one of those orange pallet carts you see contractors rolling around the lumber section at seven a.m. every day. The cart was flush with her bumper so as not to stick out into the parking lot and impede other drivers. That's the kind of considerate person Bonnie is.

As she had done since her PTSD diagnosis, she brought her therapy dog, a German Shepherd, along with her. She had the dog by her side. She couldn't load the trunk with the pallet cart in her way *and* her dog on her arm, however, so she put him into his kennel in the backseat of the car and shifted the cart to the side. As soon as the dog was safely stowed and she'd closed the rear passenger door, she heard a voice from behind.

"Hey there, can I help you with that?"

"No, no, I'm fine, thank you. I have everything." And she did. Bonnie is petite, but she is also a strong woman. A forty-pound bag of potting soil is no problem for her.

There was a moment of silence. And—given Bonnie's past experiences with violence, combined with the innate sense most have for those moments when something doesn't feel quite right—probably sheer terror. I can never know the thoughts and emotions that raced through her head, but I would imagine they began with the word, *Again?!*

Suddenly, the man offering help grabbed Bonnie around the waist and picked her up. Her purse, which held her gun, slid off her shoulder and fell to the ground. Her dog began to bark wildly, but he was stuck in his cage, in a closed car. Neither was of any use.

Much the way Sara described the instantaneous thought process she went through when she woke up to find a strange man on top of her in her dorm room, Bonnie described a sort of checklist she went down as her petite frame hung suspended in the air.

I can't get to my gun.

I don't have mace.

My dog is locked up.

*What are my other options?**

Being much smaller than the man who now had a hold of her, the top of her head was barely at his chin level. You might not think that being shorter than your attacker could be an advantage in a violent encounter, but in this case, it was. Bonnie realized that her arms had a much greater range of motion down lower than if he'd hoisted her so her head was above his. She immediately considered how to put this counterintuitive advantage into play.

I can get to his neck.

Bonnie torqued her torso, folded her arm into a V so her elbow was as pointed as possible, and untwisted like a corkscrew in one smooth, lightning-quick motion, ramming her elbow into the man's throat as hard as she could.

The blow forced the attacker to release his grip on Bonnie and drew his attention instinctively to the site of the trauma as he reeled backward, unsteadily.

Having gone through our training twice, Bonnie knew that the encounter was likely not over. Or even close to over. She had the advantage, but how long would it last? The man was still mobile. He was still her opponent and would be until he was deprived of the ability to move. She had to use her advantage to the fullest.

What else can I get?

Staggered, his hands around his throat, the man's lower body was vulnerable. He wasn't thinking about his legs at this point—not as weapons or a means of escape or, unlike Bonnie, as targets.

---

* If I deserve any credit, I am proud my training contributed to that thought. A victim does not think they have options. They submit.

I can get his knee.

She took a step, planted on her left leg, and stomped straight down through his kneecap with the heel of the shoe on her right foot until she heard a pop. He screamed in agony and collapsed to the ground, completely incapacitated. The whole thing took less than twenty seconds. A few minutes later, the police arrived, the man was cuffed, and Bonnie was safe.

After the incident, the police went back through footage from the surveillance cameras in the parking lot. It quickly became apparent that Bonnie's attacker had planned his assault. His van was nearby—unlocked and running. He had been circling the parking lot for some time, looking for a victim. When he spotted Bonnie, he figured her for an easy target. He was bigger, faster, and stronger, and she didn't look like someone who'd fight back. She was petite, she had her hands full, she seemed distracted. So he made his move.

But looking like a victim and *being* a victim are very different things. Whatever his perceptions had been, the man was no match for Bonnie. When he tried to pick her up, his fantasy met the full, sharp-elbowed force of her reality. Bonnie knew exactly what to do, not because she was an expert martial artist, but because she had studied the tool of violence.

Bonnie knew that the human body comes equipped with bypass points—*targets*—where a focused effort can negate an assailant's size, speed, and strength. When she was faced with real asocial violence, her emotional baggage and hesitation took a backseat to the fact that, in this moment, the only way to flip the situation in her favor was to put trauma on one of her assailant's bypass points.

What's available to me? How can I injure him?

Those were her first thoughts, and they were the right ones.

They helped her immediately identify her attacker's most accessible target (the throat) and then spot another vulnerability (the knee) once the initial trauma had been inflicted. She did not stop after one blow—she followed through. Those two injuries, back-to-back, produced a non-functional attacker. If only for a moment, she became the attacker she had been so reluctant to be in our first session together. Fortunately, it was the right moment—the moment between life and death.

Bonnie's ability to identify accessible targets, and to do it in an instant, gave her an advantage. Her appreciation for the fact that when you're facing violence in real life, you may not get to pick your target, and you may not get to pick your tools, saved Bonnie's life. Her dog was locked up, her gun was out of reach, and she was being restrained by her assailant, but none of that mattered. None of it could stop her from identifying accessible targets and inflicting an injury.

But what exactly is a target? And what is an injury? We've already talked a bit about how the presence of natural vulnerabilities in the human body—*every* human body—is the great leveler when it comes to violence. Now, we're going to dive into those vulnerabilities in more detail; I'll spend the rest of this chapter equipping you with the information and tools you need to identify and disable as many of those targets as necessary when your life is at stake.

IF IT BREAKS, IT'S A TARGET

A target is an anatomical structure that can be crushed, ruptured, broken, or otherwise rendered useless, thereby rendering your opponent useless.

Full stop.

That is the definition of a target. Read it again. It's simple, but there are some hard concepts and visceral images associated with the words in that definition. Reread them until they don't make you wince, until they are simply facts. Equally as important as getting comfortable with this concept is becoming familiar with the *characteristics* of those targets that generalize across the human body. The more familiar you get with them, the faster you're able to identify what you can get in the heat of the moment, and the easier it is to embrace what your job is once you do.

Targets are places that are critical to normal functioning. The eyes, the throat, the genitals, joints, motor nerves, just to name a few. These are the structures the body can't do without if it's going to run around and function at peak performance. You can punch someone in the stomach or kick them in the butt and it can be painful, but it won't incapacitate the victim because the area of trauma is non-critical and non-specific. Some of these areas are more vulnerable than others, and require different angles or amounts of force, but they are all critical for normal human function—walking, breathing, seeing, grabbing things—which means they are critical to stopping your attacker.

Targets are the entry point for a vector of force. Most people imagine a target as a point, a circle or dot that could be drawn on the skin that means "hit here." A target is *not* simply a dot on the skin around the critical, injury-prone area. It's not the pointy part of the Adam's apple or the round part of the kneecap or the iris of the eye.

This is really, really important. If you get nothing else from this section, remember this: a target is an aim-point through which you are going to visualize putting *all* your body weight, with the goal of creating an entry wound. And every decent entry wound has an exit wound, with a tunnel of wreckage between the two. This is what bullets do and it's what you must visualize yourself doing (more on this later). You are going to throw yourself through the target, to make whatever tool you're using come out the other side, whether it's your thumb, like in Sara's case, your boot heel, like with Bonnie, or your fist, like Jorge Orozco.

When you look at a target, your mindset should be biased toward action and your point of view should be set to a three-dimensional, vector-infested picture of your attacker's anatomy. You should be looking into the future, through the tunnel of wreckage you are about to create, visualizing where your enemy has folded and broken from the injury you are about to inflict. Bonnie didn't just hit the surface of her assailant's kneecap, she struck it as if she could drive her heel all the way through it, pinning him to the concrete like the tail onto the donkey. That degree of force, and the visualization behind it, made the difference between hurting her assailant and injuring him to the point of incapacitation.

Targets are places where injuries occur. There are parts of the body that are most prone to injury when human beings collide with each other or with the ground. One way to learn about these natural targets is to pay close attention to combat sports like boxing or MMA, and contact sports like football or rugby, where these collisions most often occur. Sports have less to teach us about real-world violence than you might think—they're governed by rules in ways that real, life-or-death encounters never are—but they do have something to teach us about the vulnerabilities in the human body. They are a rich source of injury data.

Sure, sports injuries are still delivered under artificial circumstances by highly trained athletes—but the human bodies on the line are fundamentally the same as human bodies anywhere. The forces that caused these injuries are forces you and I can replicate if we need to defend ourselves, so they're applicable for our purposes.

In 2004, Bernard Hopkins and Oscar De La Hoya met in Las Vegas for a unification bout that would finally decide the undisputed middleweight champion of the world. Hopkins was 45-2-1, De La Hoya was 37-3. The promoters billed the fight as "History," and it would live up to its name.

Like many fights between evenly matched fighters, this one started out slow. Over the first eight rounds, they fought a fairly boring, tactical fight, not doing much damage to each other. Going into the ninth round, Hopkins was ahead on two judges' scorecards, De La Hoya was slightly ahead on the other's. Coming out at the bell, Hopkins finally took the initiative and started pressing De La Hoya, getting aggressive. Hopkins found his way inside and started working angles, moving De La Hoya around the ring. Then, at almost exactly the halfway point of the round, Hopkins delivered a picture-perfect left hook to the lower margin of De La Hoya's right rib cage. It was so quick you could barely see it.

De La Hoya's body froze up, his eyes got lazy, then he folded over and dropped to the canvas writhing in agony. He pressed his gloved hands into the canvas, with his head between them, like he was praying for the pain to stop. He made no effort at all to respond to the ten-count being issued by the referee two feet above his head. He probably couldn't hear the count over the sound of his brain sending its focus to the right side of his abdomen. Hopkins had just leveled De La Hoya with a textbook liver punch. If a boxer can slip through his opponent's defenses, it's one of the most devastating punches he can deliver.

In their entire careers up to that moment—eighty-eight combined fights—Hopkins had never knocked a man out and De La Hoya had never been knocked out. In this fight alone, they'd exchanged and weathered hundreds of jabs, hooks, crosses, and uppercuts. Yet with a single well-placed body shot in close quarters, Hopkins brought down De La Hoya like a sack of potatoes.

Of course, De La Hoya wanted to keep fighting. He wanted to win—but he physically couldn't. In that moment, his brain had been taken out of the equation. He couldn't will his body into action. He was dealing with totally incapacitating injury, one that was telling his brain to shut everything down, to focus all available resources on the damaged zone and forget about anything more complicated. For Oscar De La Hoya, it was his very first knockout blow; for us, it's data on a vulnerable part of the body.

Over all my years of watching and studying combat sports, sports injury data has proved to be a treasure trove of insight when it comes to understanding exactly *where* to use the tool of violence against a bigger, stronger, faster adversary. What you learn is that just trying to hit an adversary hard wherever you can reach is almost never the best approach. Heavy force to a specifically vulnerable area should be the goal.

Joe Theismann's famously gruesome broken leg on Monday Night Football in 1985 is a quintessential example: Lawrence Taylor brought the full force of his body through a weak spot in Theismann's planted front leg and snapped it like a tree branch. Theismann went down in a heap and never played football again. Of course, LT was one of the greatest athletes to ever play football—but you don't need to be a great athlete to destroy a knee like that. A knee is a knee is a knee. The force that destroyed Theismann's knee was a force you and I can easily replicate with proper leverage and intent. That is the force of injury.

It might surprise you to learn that this is just how the military thinks about inflicting harm, even with its most sophisticated weapons. As military technology improves, our bombs and munitions haven't gotten bigger—they've gotten smaller. It's our targeting that has gotten better. We're increasingly able to put explosives exactly where we want—in the most vulnerable part of the enemy's defenses. There's a lot to be learned from that. Just ask the members of the Mexican Mafia I discussed in Chapter Four, who study and learn the vulnerabilities of the human body, and understand that a 250-pound martial artist has the same inherent vulnerabilities as a twelve-year-old girl. Violent criminals already think in terms of targets, and when they need to, they can incapacitate those targets in brutal fashion.

Injuries of the kinds we've been discussing—ones like the kind that disabled De La Hoya and Theismann, and stopped them in their tracks—turn up again and again in the sports medicine literature. Most of us (especially in the United States) already know this, whether we realize it or not. From football alone, we've watched players laid out on the turf gasping desperately for air after a hit to the solar plexus. We've sat breathless ourselves as defenders lay motionless with neck stingers after traumatic high-velocity collisions in that exposed region between the bottom of the helmet and the top of the shoulder pads. We have a kinesiologist-level understanding of the structure of the knee—ACL, MCL, LCL, patella tendon, meniscus—thanks to years of watching running backs collapse to the turf in heaps after planting wrong or taking a hit from the wrong angle. If you're looking for a list of places to incapacitate a person much bigger and stronger than you, you could do much worse than the Injured Reserve list for a typical NFL team.

Everything stops on the field when these injuries occur, right? It's not so different out in the real world. When Bonnie struck her assailant in the throat, it was only enough to get herself free. It wasn't until she sent a disproportionate amount of force through his knee ligaments at the optimal angle that he was truly incapacitated and the action stopped.

Another way to think of this is that targets are "virtual injuries"—places that are injuries just waiting to happen, that you can visualize when you think about them in three dimensions. The "knee target" is a potential broken knee, bent backward or sideways, until it makes a loud, bad sound. It's falling and not being able to get back up. The "spleen target" is broken ribs and a bruised (or ruptured) organ. It's the inability to breathe and internal bleeding that can lead to shock. If direct trauma to your target cannot produce a similar kind of incapacitating injury, then it is not a target.

We started this section with a definition; let's end it with a full description. Targets are entry points for maximum force at places on the body that are critical for normal functioning and are often prone to injury.

Just remember: they don't become injuries until you make them so.

WHAT TARGETS *AREN'T*

Just as important as understanding what a target is at a practical and an anatomical level, is knowing what a target *isn't*.

Targets are not "weak points." To say that targets are "weak points" is to imply that it is easier to break them than other areas of the body. This point of view conflates weakness and vulnerability. Just because something is more vulnerable does not mean it's any less difficult to injure. Time and again I see this fundamental misunderstanding lead some of my students to give less than their all when they train to attack particular regions of the body. Whether you're lacerating a cornea or tearing a hip out of its socket, it's going to take everything you have, if for no other reason than humans are wired to aggressively defend those places we instinctively know are more vulnerable. When bracing for a car collision, for instance, our instinct is to shield our faces in the moments prior to impact. We do this reflexively, even when we know that trauma to the eyes and face are never the causes of death in fatalities. The same general rule applies to violent confrontation, which means to use anything less than the full force of your effort is deadly stupidity. Your attacker has no plans to pull his punches, so neither should you.

By the same token, thinking of targets as "weak points" implies that if only you could strengthen them, you could make yourself impervious to harm. Let me be very clear about this: there is no amount of size, strength, or speed that can make what we have defined here as a target *not a target.* Not for you, not for your opponent, not for anyone. Dwayne "The Rock" Johnson has massive forearms and biceps. In between them is an elbow joint that is roughly the same size as any other grown man's elbow joint. And it snaps the same way with roughly the same amount of force if you wrench it the wrong way. No amount of bicep curls is going to change that fact.

Take the human skull. It is perpetually vulnerable in violent confrontations, but that doesn't mean it's weak. The skull is resilient, flexible, and hard as all get-out. It takes a considerable application of force to create an incapacitating injury—whether that's the force of concrete and gravity, or a tire iron, or something as simple (and ancient) as a stone in the hand. You have to give it your all. Just ask Goliath. Or rather ask David, since he won that famous little confrontation despite the overwhelming size and strength disparity.

Targets are not "pressure points." Thinking of targets as "pressure points" implies that simple pressure (pushing, pinching, squeezing, or poking) will produce the desired effect. Does it hurt to have any of those things happen to a target? That kind of thing might work when rough-housing with a sibling as a kid, or on television if your name is Mr. Spock, but in the real world the difference between pain and injury is an insurmountable gulf. When it comes to incapacitating your opponent—to breaking physical structures or shutting off sensory systems—"pressure points" are a myth. Each condition can exist independent of the other, and while pain can be a result of injury, injury is never the result of pain or pressure. Injury is the result of trauma, of breakage and the tunnel of wreckage you endeavor to create through the entry point that every true target represents. Whether something "hurts" your opponent is irrelevant; what matters is whether it breaks and incapacitates.

Poking a "pressure point" gets you nothing. Giving it your all gets you everything.

THERE IS NO TOP TEN LIST

Asocial violence is random, and it's unpredictable. Survival is its test. To pass the test, you must understand its underlying principles. A list of facts and a few neat tricks and shortcuts will rarely be enough, because things rarely ever go the way you want them to. If they did, you wouldn't have to know all this stuff in the first place, now would you?

And yet, the most common question I get from new students and seminar attendees is: "What are the top three places on the body to cause an injury?" In a lot of self-defense literature and instruction you will read or hear about the big three: *eyes, groin, throat.* And indeed those are three targets on the human body, but to say those are the "top three" is a dangerous mindset based on a faulty premise.

First, it assumes there is some kind of list sortable by magnitude of damage or effort required or size disparity—like a matrix. More critically, it presupposes full access to the opponent's body. And in a case of real-world violence, there's no guarantee that you're going to have that. Bonnie sure didn't.

Neither did another of my students, whom I will call Shawn.

Shawn is a doctor. One day after his shift, he went to the grocery store to pick up some things for the week ahead.

Much like Bonnie, he was attacked in the parking lot while loading items into the backseat of his car. When he straightened himself to shut the door, out of nowhere he felt the barrel of a .45 caliber pistol pressed against his right temple. It was dark, and it wasn't immediately clear where the man was positioned in relation to Shawn's body, so he needed a second to get his bearings. Frozen in place, Shawn caught a glimpse of the man's shoe pointing in his direction. Immediately, Shawn recognized that the man was on the other side of the car door, that there was a shield between them, and that the man's foot was his vulnerable target.

Shawn dropped, directing his body weight through his right knee into the joint where the attacker's ankle meets his foot. It was a textbook knee-drop. By doing this, Shawn compounded his chances of survival by clearing his head from the trajectory of the gun as he simultaneously inflicted an injury. The knee-drop broke a bunch of bones in the man's foot, causing him to instinctively reach down and drop his gun. Shawn then quickly grabbed the back of the man's heel and pulled it toward him, using the car door as both shield — from the upper half of the man's body in case he had another weapon — and leverage, bracing himself against it to pull the attacker to the ground. Now with the man's entire leg exposed under the car door, Shawn re-secured his grip on the man's foot and thrust the lower leg up into the bottom of the car door, shattering it. The blinding shock of trauma caused the man to pass out. Finally, Shawn called the police.

When Shawn felt the gun against his head, most of his body was shielded by the car door... *but so was the attacker's body*. His groin was behind metal and glass, and his eyes and throat were well out of reach. If Shawn only knew how to inflict injury on the "big three" targets, he would have been in trouble. That's why I don't give my students a rote list of targets to memorize. I give them tools and teach them principles to identify the best, most vulnerable target at any given moment, to help them quickly figure out their own answers. Those tools include asking the right questions:

- Can I reach the target?
- Can I disable it with my bare hands?
- From my position, can I generate enough force to cause severe injury to the target?
- If I injure it, what ability do I strip from my opponent?
- Will injuring it be enough to shut down my opponent's command center?

The chain of events that resulted in Shawn's survival began with a knee-drop to the top of the foot. As targets go, the foot is not as sexy as the eyes, throat, or groin. "Smash the guy's left foot" is not going to appear on any listicle or YouTube self-defense video you may encounter. In the movies, you rarely see the hero go for the foot in the climactic "all is lost" moment when he's at the mercy of the villain and needs to seize the initiative. Instead, you most often see the foot targeted in cartoons, as a punch line. The little guy pulls out a mallet and slams it down on the big guy's foot, then the injured guy hops around on one leg and everyone laughs.

Those jokes have a kernel of truth to them: in reality, the foot is a great target. It's full of bones and ligaments, which are wrapped in nerves. Foot-whipping has been a popular form of corporal punishment for hundreds of years because of the hyper-sensitivity of the plantar fascia tendon and the nerve endings that run along the longitudinal arch of the human foot. As a doctor, Shawn had a deep understanding of anatomy like that. He knew all this about the human foot. He knew that the top of the foot was full of small bones connecting to the ankle, where you can fairly easily create a disproportionate effect (i.e., excruciating trauma that destroys the integrity of the foot) in relation to the amount of force required.

In addition to knowing that the top of his attacker's foot was a viable target, Shawn recognized that it was his *only* target. It was the most accessible area on his body given their physical orientation. Going after it allowed him to move his head out of the path of the gun at the same time. If he inflicted an injury to the area, he also figured he'd gain access to other targets as a result. So he went for it.

Shawn started with a single strike, and once he seized the initiative, he continued to incapacitate his attacker. But he was not successful because he'd trained his strikes as a series of techniques related to an armed robbery or carjacking scenario. He succeeded because he'd trained to identify targets and to internalize the mindset that your best targets are the ones you can get, and you go after each one in turn with the intent to create a tunnel of wreckage until your attacker is incapacitated.

That's the difference between someone who understands the principles of violence and someone who only understands techniques. Shawn knew the same eye-gouging technique as Sara and the same throat strike as Bonnie. Had his focus been solely on those techniques he would have been looking for specific targets that weren't available to him, to the exclusion of the opportunities that his principles exposed. It would have been a fatal mistake.

THINK LIKE A BULLET

Identify targets. Act first. Give it everything you have. Those principles are *what* you should be thinking about when it comes to asocial violence. But *how* should you be thinking about them? It's a seemingly complicated question with a surprisingly simple answer:

Think like a bullet.

A bullet flies straight, fast, and true. It goes in, through, and out the other side of whatever stands in its way. That should be how you think about applying the principles of violence in a life-or-death situation. If you can do it, it makes everything simpler. It simplifies an ethically complicated issue. It strips away the kind of emotional and moral baggage that held Bonnie back initially. It eliminates the kind of hesitation that nearly cost Officer Jeter her life.

It also makes learning, training, and perfecting the tool of violence much easier.

At one of our evening training sessions in San Diego several years ago, a young Navy corpsman* dropped in unannounced with less than an hour left in the session. Someone told her that we could teach her to fight "like they do in prison" and she really wanted to learn. Under normal circumstances

---

* A corpsman is a medical specialist who often works in hospitals while stationed on base and provides on-site medical care to units deployed in the field.

we would have asked her to come to the next class, but we were so taken by her enthusiasm that we decided to go for it and see what we could do in forty-five minutes.

San Diego isn't as crazy as it was in the 1980s when my buddy Mike nearly lost his life on the other end of an ex-con's switchblade, but it still has its tough parts, especially for a woman. Plus, if she ever got deployed into an active war zone, she needed to know how to handle herself, while at the same time taking care of the soldiers in her unit. We could tell this woman was a fire-eater, and that is a huge advantage when it comes to learning, absorbing, and training the tool of violence. It means less time explaining the little things that often only matter at the margins, and more time focused on the fundamental things that produce the biggest returns.

The class was turned over to another instructor and we got to work with the corpsman. When I began my career as an instructor, I found that it took more than a week for my students to get a handle on the material and get ready to simulate inflicting real violence. It took that long to get them to "unlearn" the rules of social aggression that don't apply in a fight for your life, and to get their mindsets to the point at which they could really visualize doing real harm to an adversary. As I grew as an instructor over the years, I refined my methods and delivery systems for all the key information and found that, by focusing intensively on mindset first, I could compress the key points into as little as ninety minutes. And now we were going to give it a go in half that time.

The good news was that, as a trained medical professional, the corpsman knew her way around anatomy and debilitating injury. We didn't have to explain to her how a body breaks or what an injury is. That helped shave off a good chunk of work. On top of that, as a trained member of the military she had no problems throwing herself into the mix. She wasn't quite thinking like a bullet—more like an unguided missile—but with focused work on tools and targets, we dialed in her aim in no time.

We assembled the eye target I use to show my students how to deliver a proper gouge, using the thumb, fingers, and heel depending on the orientation of the attacker— standing, kneeling, and on the ground. Then we worked on the neck, breaking it and crushing the throat, again from all orientations—vertical to horizontal. After that, we attacked the groin target—rupturing testicles with elbows, knees, and boots from all angles. And finally, we went through the principles for breaking ankles from the front, side, and behind.

Then we demonstrated how to string these injuries together, one after the other, leaving the exact sequence up to the corpsman: gouge an eye, put a boot through the groin, break an ankle, then stomp the throat. Or fist through the groin, forearm hammer through the back of the neck, gouge the eye.

It didn't really matter, we told the corpsman. What mattered was putting herself all the way through each target to wreck it, then picking the next one and repeating the process until she was satisfied that her attacker would be non-functional. What mattered was thinking like a bullet whose force is self-directed and self-controlled.

We were done with this part in thirty minutes. For the last fifteen minutes of class we left her to her own devices with a training partner. She took to it with the same fire and enthusiasm she walked in the door with.

I know that most students won't take to this material as quickly as that corpsman did, and that's fine. But some of what made the material so intuitive for her will work just as well for any student. What works is *simplicity*. Protecting yourself in life-or-death situations is fundamentally simple, and we only waste time by adding complications. That's the difference between training to learn techniques and training to learn principles. And that's why I tell my students to think like a bullet: set your intent, remove complications from your mind, and go straight through the target you can get.

TO INJURE OR NOT TO INJURE

Most people, especially untrained people, see the different means of inflicting injury as a progression, as a scale extending from least effective to most effective. Bare hands are, in this way of thinking, the least effective means at our disposal, because they require more direct physical effort on our part. Impact weapons (sticks, clubs, bats, batons) and knives are better. Firearms are the end-all be-all, because they prepackage the requirements for injury and require nothing more than a trigger-pull and a moderately clear shot to get the job done. One, two, three. Big, bigger, biggest. Good, better, best. The progression feels natural.

There is another way of thinking about violence, however, which is far better suited to equipping the average person with a weapon that is impossible to disarm. This way of thinking dispenses with shades of gray and exists only in the binary world of black and white. In this world, there is either injury or there is no injury. That's it.

The mindset I am trying to instill in you is unconcerned with *the means* of inflicting injury, it's only concerned with whether you are successful. In this way, a firearm isn't the goal, or the end of the line, but rather just an excellent *example* of what is required in the successful execution of life-saving violence. If you don't have a handgun, that's fine. All that matters is that you end up at the same place: on the other side of a tunnel of wreckage.

That's why your goal is really to be able to do the work of a bullet—to injure a critical target, to incapacitate—with your bare hands. In a life-or-death struggle, you want to be able to effect the same end result whether you shot him, stabbed him, broke him with a stick or "just" your bare hands.

We've discussed how to think about causing injury quite a bit—but all of this may come into greater focus for you if we give some more thought to exactly what an injury is, and what it does to the injured person. What, exactly, does it mean to "injure" someone?

Our bodies have built-in systems for responding to physical trauma. When a trauma stimulus is triggered in the body, the sensory impulses are delivered to and from the brain via what are called the afferent and efferent nervous systems. At one point or another, we've all experienced mild versions of these "knee jerk" reactions—flinching when being tickled, or yanking our hand away from a hot stove, for instance. In cases of severe trauma, our bodies will react before conscious thought even kicks in, inducing a spinal reflex reaction that occupies the brain and takes away our power to choose how to react (this is how the liver punch in boxing and MMA is so incapacitating).

I can't stress it enough: in self-protection, our goal is not to block or prevent this kind of damage to our own bodies as much as it is to exploit these reactions in our opponents' bodies and inflict disabling trauma whenever necessary, wherever possible. We can't give the enemy the choice to fight through the pain and use adrenaline to continue attacking. We need to incapacitate him.

Where are some of the specific areas that easily trigger spinal reflex reactions? We've already heard stories about attacking the eyes and the throat and the tops of the feet. We've discussed the joints — elbows, knees, ankles — as prime targets, as well. Remarkably, there are more than *seventy* anatomical areas on the human body that can trigger the same incapacitating reflex if injured.*

Inflicting enough trauma on any of these areas will shut down the brain or, at the very minimum, occupy it with the site of trauma to the exclusion of effectuating its prior will to attack you. When the ability to make that choice — or any decisions at all, frankly — is stripped from your enemy, he becomes a sitting duck. Take the brain away, and it no longer matters that your opponent is bigger or faster or stronger, or if he's a jiujitsu master or an MMA practitioner, or if he's skilled at using a knife or a gun. Without a brain, he's helpless.

That is what it means to injure and incapacitate.

A reactive, hesitant person locked into a victim's mindset does not see the empowerment that can be derived from the understanding of how injury works. Instead, he looks at the array of violence survival methods we've touched on in this chapter and fixates on their differences. He sees a gradient

---

* There is a diagram and full list of targets on the following page, for reference.

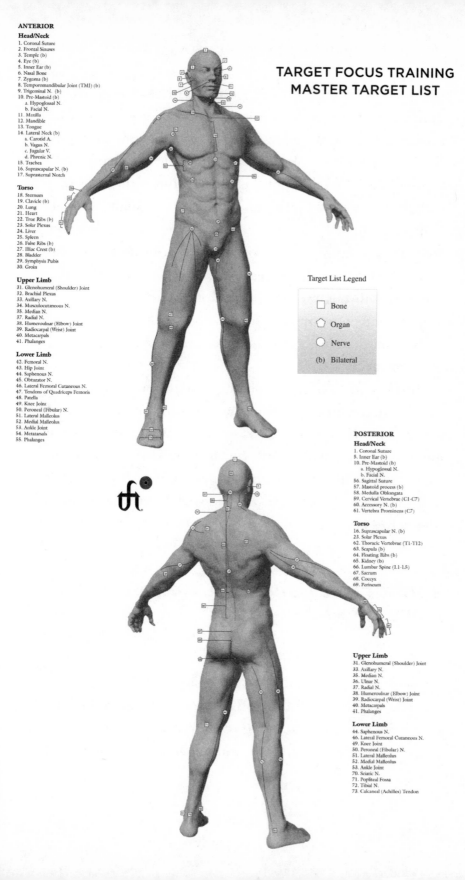

TARGET FOCUS TRAINING
MASTER TARGET LIST

ANTERIOR

Head/Neck
1. Coronal Suture
2. Frontal Sinuses
3. Temple (b)
4. Eye (b)
5. Inner Ear (b)
6. Nasal Bone
7. Zygoma (b)
8. Temporomandibular Joint (TMJ) (b)
9. Trigeminal N. (b)
10. Pre-Mastoid (b)
   a. Hypoglossal N.
   b. Facial N.
11. Maxilla
12. Mandible
13. Tongue
14. Lateral Neck (b)
   a. Carotid A.
   b. Vagus N.
   c. Jugular V.
   d. Phrenic N.
15. Trachea
16. Suprascapular N. (b)
17. Suprasternal Notch

Torso
18. Sternum
19. Clavicle (b)
20. Lung
21. Heart
22. True Ribs (b)
23. Solar Plexus
24. Liver
25. Spleen
26. False Ribs (b)
27. Iliac Crest (b)
28. Bladder
29. Symphysis Pubis
30. Groin

Upper Limb
31. Glenohumeral (Shoulder) Joint
32. Brachial Plexus
33. Axillary N.
34. Musculocutaneous N.
35. Median N.
37. Radial N.
38. Humeroulnar (Elbow) Joint
39. Radiocarpal (Wrist) Joint
40. Metacarpals
41. Phalanges

Lower Limb
42. Femoral N.
43. Hip Joint
44. Saphenous N.
45. Obturator N.
46. Lateral Femoral Cutaneous N.
47. Tendons of Quadriceps Femoris
48. Patella
49. Knee Joint
50. Peroneal (Fibular) N.
51. Lateral Malleolus
52. Medial Malleolus
54. Ankle Joint
54. Metatarsals
55. Phalanges

Target List Legend
☐ Bone
⬠ Organ
◯ Nerve
(b) Bilateral

POSTERIOR

Head/Neck
1. Coronal Suture
5. Inner Ear (b)
10. Pre-Mastoid (b)
   a. Hypoglossal N.
   b. Facial N.
56. Sagittal Suture
57. Mastoid process (b)
58. Medulla Oblongata
59. Cervical Vertebrae (C1-C7)
60. Accessory N. (b)
61. Vertebra Prominens (C7)

Torso
16. Suprascapular N. (b)
23. Solar Plexus
62. Thoracic Vertebrae (T1-T12)
63. Scapula (b)
64. Floating Ribs (b)
65. Kidney (b)
66. Lumbar Spine (L1-L5)
67. Sacrum
68. Coccyx
69. Perineum

Upper Limb
31. Glenohumeral (Shoulder) Joint
33. Axillary N.
35. Median N.
36. Ulnar N.
37. Radial N.
38. Humeroulnar (Elbow) Joint
39. Radiocarpal (Wrist) Joint
40. Metacarpals
41. Phalanges

Lower Limb
44. Saphenous N.
46. Lateral Femoral Cutaneous N.
49. Knee Joint
50. Peroneal (Fibular) N.
51. Lateral Malleolus
52. Medial Malleolus
53. Ankle Joint
70. Sciatic N.
71. Popliteal Fossa
72. Tibial N.
73. Calcaneal (Achilles) Tendon

of effort and difficulty, and with it a whole host of nasty things that might go wrong in between each method if he tries, as I suggest throughout this book, to create an injury and short-circuit his assailant's brain. This is because he is focused on the means, not the ends. And it is the ends that make every method, every target, and every injury similar. Achieving those ends is based on striking with a singular goal: incapacitation and survival. The correct means to that end are delivery of the largest amount of kinetic energy you can muster through vulnerable anatomy. The knife, the stick, and the ends of your skeleton are all driven by your entire mass in motion, just as the bullet is driven by energy stored in chemical bonds.

If you know what you're doing, striking someone with a fist or a boot can do an equivalent amount of damage and achieve the same desired result as a bullet fired from the most advanced weapon. All that matters is that you direct your energy fully and without hesitation, not at some idealized list of optimal targets, but at whichever ones present themselves in the moment.

BIGGER, FASTER, STRONGER, ARMED: IT DOESN'T MATTER

It's not about being the biggest and strongest on the block. *If you know what you're doing*—that's the key. It's about applying your knowledge and training. This has been a central theme of the book: when it comes to real-life violence, the natural physical advantages of those who are bigger, stronger, and faster can always be mitigated by those who have the right knowledge and aren't afraid to use it.

Of course, I'd rather be healthy and strong than the alternative. I'd rather have a size, strength, and speed advantage—it would be disingenuous and foolish to say those aren't assets in the realm of violence. They can help you absorb non-specific trauma—in other words, "take a punch." They can help you in a life-or-death fight when your enemy screws up and strikes you but fails to injure you. They might also serve as a deterrent to an attacker and a source of confidence to their holder. But the advantages stop there, because no one, no matter how big, strong, fast, or tough they are, can take injury as we define it (or as the criminal sociopath defines it). No one can take a gouged eye, a crushed throat, or a broken leg.

When football players like Joe Theismann get their leg bent backward until the bones snap, we see elite athletes suffering game-ending, and maybe career-ending, injuries. If bigger-stronger-faster conferred immunity to physical harm, football players would have it. But they don't. They break just like the rest of us.

Does being bigger, stronger, and faster help you inflict injury? Sure, but again only up to a point. If you lack the knowledge to identify available targets and the training to inflict serious, immediate harm, those physical advantages are a wash. A violent predator with a goal can handle more, bigger bruises to non-critical regions of his body from someone who doesn't know what they're doing because he knows his opportunity to make the decisive blow will make itself known soon enough.

Fortunately, the same rule applies when the shoe is on

the other foot. If your attacker has a size, speed, and strength advantage, there's still nothing he can do to protect himself from *you,* if you know what you're doing and you can do it better and faster than him. He might be able to "take a punch," but you're not going to punch him. You're going to gouge out his eye, crush his throat, and snap the connective tissue in his knee. You're going to do the things to him that nobody can take and they are going to work because he breaks just like you, just like me, just like a professional football player, just like anyone else.

When it comes to trauma to the human body, all men and women really are created equal. Maybe the most remarkable thing about targets is that everyone has them, and that they render everyone equally vulnerable.

My own story is the epitome of this universal truth that our human body is a great equalizer. An infection and a burst eardrum nearly killed me and ultimately ended my SEAL career. At that point in my life, I was the epitome of bigger, faster, and stronger. I was in my early twenties, and I was arrogant. I thought I was invincible. But when that wave of water incapacitated me in a matter of seconds, I was truly humbled. It changed the way I looked at violence forever.

Just think about the implications of our biology in the world of asocial violence. Our universal vulnerability means that the most comforting traditional notions we have about violence aren't true: that we can reliably protect ourselves by being big and strong, or by being armed; that we can easily identify threats on sight; that if we're *not* big and strong, there's little point to learning about the tool of violence at all, because we're doomed to failure from the outset. Accepting what I'm telling you here means throwing those notions out the window. It means that anyone can inflict serious harm on anyone else, and that the real edge goes to the person with the willingness and the training to get the job done.

TURNING THE ODDS IN YOUR FAVOR

Independent of any physical, intellectual, or practical advantage, the reality of asocial violence is that your chances of survival at the beginning of a confrontation, before the first injury, are just about fifty-fifty. A coin flip. It doesn't matter who you are, these odds apply to everyone — even myself.

I've been training for violence my entire adult life. I'm very good at what I do. I understand exactly how to use the tool of violence. If I am threatened and stripped of my ability to escape or de-escalate, I won't hesitate. I will be the first to attack. Yet, I walk around every day with no more than a fifty-fifty chance of getting it right. Because if I'm facing another person with an active brain, that person could think and move against me. If I haven't disconnected the will of his brain from the movement of his body via injury, I am perpetually at risk. I am not immune from the principles I am trying to teach you. They work just as well on me as they do on violent criminals — which is precisely what makes them so valuable and so important to learn.

These odds that I'm describing apply at the *outset* of a violent confrontation. It's what happens once the confrontation starts — whether we choose to act or react, whether we can stay in Cause Mode and effectively consign our opponent to Effect Mode — that can shift the odds in our favor as the encounter develops. If you're truly prepared to do what it takes to protect yourself, most of your attacker's neutralizing advantages begin to disappear.

One of my clients is a neurosurgeon.* We'll call him Peter. Late at night, Peter was called in to an inner-city hospital to treat a young child — an eight-year-old boy who needed immediate brain surgery to survive. Walking from his car, Peter was randomly attacked by two men. The first guy had a knife. Peter saw the knife and was able to slam his ulna (pinky side of the forearm) into the first attacker's radial nerve (that runs from the palm-side of the thumb to the elbow). The criminal's hand opened and he dropped the knife. Peter then threw his ulna into the guy's neck, which whipped the man's head forward and gave him a concussion as he fell to the ground. At that point, the other assailant ran off.

Hospital security officers arrived to detain the first attacker, who was completely knocked out, and Peter ran inside to perform the surgery. After saving the young boy's life in the emergency room, Peter washed up and wrote me a note. He told me, interestingly, that it wasn't his superior knowledge of anatomy as a trained physician that made the difference, it was that he didn't have to think about what to do as he was being attacked, because he was trained in targets and the tool of violence.

He saw a clear path to survival — the knowledge of which began to tip the odds in Peter's favor before he even made

---

* Doctors make up a sizable portion of my client base for several reasons: they are high-status individuals who drive nice cars and wear nice watches; they are often blamed by the families of deceased patients; and they work in hospitals that are often situated in urban areas with elevated crime rates.

his first move. When he took the initiative and went on the attack, the odds tilted more. They tilted even further when he disarmed the attacker. And once he incapacitated the man, the odds were entirely on his side, which the assailant's partner recognized.

But here's the key point: until Peter identified the available targets and effectively inflicted the incapacitating injuries, the odds were even and the outcome was uncertain. Peter couldn't afford to let up until the scales tipped decisively in his favor. This was a very similar reality to the ones that Bonnie, restrained by her attacker, and Shawn, with a gun to his temple, were able to surmount. At the outset of the fights of their lives, before any injury had been inflicted, their odds were effectively fifty-fifty. Then, once they made their moves, it was their assailants who would have loved those even odds, because — like Peter's attackers — it was all downhill for them from that point forward.

If your number one threat is always your opponent's active brain, that means that your *own* brain is your number one weapon. It doesn't matter if the other guy has a knife or a gun. It doesn't matter if he already has his hands on you. Those are all tools and tactics that require an active brain; a brain that's able to make decisions. And the goal of any violent encounter is fundamentally the same: use your brain to shut down your opponent's brain. Bonnie, Shawn, and Peter all neutralized those tools and tactics because they shut down the enemy's command center, and because they used their own quick thinking to figure out the best way to do so. In the next chapter, then, we'll talk more about using your most effective weapon — your brain — on offense.

CHAPTER SEVEN

YOUR BRAIN IS YOUR DEADLIEST WEAPON

The human brain has 100 billion neurons, each neuron connected to ten thousand other neurons. Sitting on your shoulders is the most complicated object in the known universe.

— *Michio Kaku*

The fundamental idea of training for self-protection is to accept the reality of violence, the reality of the human body, and the reality of whatever situation you find yourself in. For many people, these are uncomfortable realities that their minds will not allow them to reconcile with their idealized vision of how the world should be. The irony is, your brain is the tool that makes that reconciliation possible. It is your best asset. Ultimately, it's the *only* weapon you'll ever truly have (or need) because it is the thing that makes everything else work. That's why we have spent so much time to this point talking about shutting down your opponent's brain and will spend this entire chapter talking about training yours.

Thirty minutes into *The Bourne Identity*, Jason Bourne and

his semi-willing accomplice, Marie, are sitting at a window table in a truck stop café somewhere between Zurich and Paris. In the twenty-four hours that have just passed, Jason, in the throes of complete amnesia, has disarmed three men, escaped an American embassy, climbed down the outside of a three-story building, and convinced Marie, a woman he has never met, to drive him to Paris by offering her $20,000. This quick meal in the café is their first break in hours and it gives them a chance to catch their breath and to take inventory of what the hell is going on. As Jason thinks out loud in front of Marie, he delivers some of the film's most famous lines:

> I can tell you the license plate numbers of all six cars outside. I can tell you that our waitress is left-handed and the guy sitting up at the counter weighs two hundred and fifteen pounds and knows how to handle himself. I know the best place to look for a gun is the cab of the gray truck outside, and at this altitude, I can run flat out for a half mile before my hands start shaking. Now why would I know that? How can I know that and not know who I am?

Granted, this is a movie—a fictional spy thriller, no less—that takes plenty of creative license as it relates to military tactics and real world hand-to-hand combat. But the essential truth that Jason's speech and the first half-hour of the movie is getting at, is the simultaneous power and vulnerability of the human brain. Deprive it of oxygen for long enough, or subject it to trauma, and it can wipe out all the information that makes you *you*. Even then, some information is ingrained so deeply, and the brain is so resilient, that it can survive almost any trauma short of death and call upon that information at a moment's notice without your conscious effort.

The power, resilience, and elasticity of the human brain have fascinated people for centuries. Today, it drives self-experimenters like Tim Ferriss, learning gurus like Jim Kwik, and start-ups like Lumosity to expand the knowledge base and capabilities of the average human being. I don't mean to place myself in such rarified company, but I am trying to do the same thing for the average person with the tool of violence. It all starts when it comes to hardening the mind to the principles and realities of violence: the brain.

The human brain is the most creative force in our universe. It has created bridges, monuments, computers, space shuttles, timeless works of art, skyscrapers, and roads that span entire continents. It's responsible for medical advances that save millions of lives every year and hundreds of millions of lives over generations.

Our brains are the reason we have been able to evolve and thrive the way we have as a species. If we had to be bigger, stronger, and faster than other predators to survive, we wouldn't be here today. The human brain allowed us to build traps and hunt in packs. We learned how to use tools. We learned how to manipulate other animals so that our size did not become a fatal evolutionary disadvantage. We made our way to the top of the food chain because we were *smarter* than all other species.

Of course, the human brain is also responsible for nuclear weapons, genocide, and heinous acts of violence. It holds tremendous power for good or for evil. In that vein, you must recognize that if you ever find yourself in a life-or-death situation, the most important asset you and your attacker bring to the confrontation will never be your physical brawn, but the creative capacity inherent in the human brain to immediately and effectively engage and channel the tool of violence.

TOTAL RECALL

I teach principles. I drill on an action-first mindset, on closing distance, identifying targets, moving with force through target vectors, and inflicting injury. Whether I see a student once for three hours on a cruise ship like Sara, for two full weekend seminars like Bonnie, or for semi-annual refresher sessions, I have a singular, overarching goal for my students: to train their brains.

Specifically, I want your brain to work on autopilot. I want it to act without the hesitation that is the hallmark of the conscious mind. In a fight for your life, after all, you are not going to be able to call timeout so you can puzzle through the list of target-identification questions I outlined in the last chapter. You won't be able to work your way through some sort of "punch here, kick there" script. That script doesn't exist, in no small part because every situation is different, but also because your opponent's brain will *already be working on autopilot* once the fight has begun. He's not going to wait for you to catch up.

This uncomfortable fact is exactly why we practice: so that we can call on automatic routines and principles when we need them the most. If you are one of the 30 percent of my students who have yet to experience real violence in your life, you may be wondering whether it is realistic to expect that, if the moment comes, you'll be able to act like Sara or Bonnie or Shawn did. And the answer is *absolutely*—if you put in the work.

Does that mean you have to spend the rest of your life sparring in training sessions or updating your knowledge in seminars? It does not—because the training process doesn't just stop when you step off the mats. Your brain continues to sort and file new ideas and new physical experiences into the buckets we construct in training: social aggression vs. asocial violence; Cause State vs. Effect State; injury vs. pain. Your understanding, familiarity, and comfort with these aspects of the tool of violence will continue to percolate days, weeks, and months after you've completed a seminar or a training session, if you allow it.

As that information simmers in your unconscious mind, it begins to hook up with your conscious understanding of the material you've learned and the muscle memory developed from the physical training you've experienced. You begin to realize that you "know" things you don't remember learning. In that sense, learning the principles of violence is like learning the principles of multiplication. You can attempt to memorize the product of countless integer combinations, and it can work for a while, but rote memorization becomes unwieldy very quickly. It also becomes unreliable when it falls out of use or the integers don't present themselves in an order you're used to seeing them in. If you learn the principles of multiplication, however, solutions to problems you've never encountered before become obvious, even when you're out of practice. When confronted with the need for action outside the training environment, your brain recognizes the commonalities between your problem and all the problems you've trained for, and recognizes the common solution. You get it, immediately. You solve. You *know*. And you act. Whether it's two numbers or two attackers.

That's the beauty of training the brain: when you practice, no matter what form that practice takes, you're always learning more than you realize. And that learning, if you allow it to sink in, results in instant, total recall in moments when you don't have time to think. It's a virtual superpower, really, and one that takes very little to begin to cultivate.

No one is better evidence for that aspect of the power of the brain than Sara. When I tell her story to audiences and new students, I don't often include the backstory I included in Chapter Two. I don't mention her similarity to Elle Woods from *Legally Blonde* or her privileged background. I use the story to convey the fact that being bigger, stronger, and faster doesn't matter and that the trained brain is the ultimate equalizer.

Often, I will have someone come up to me after I tell her story, looking for ways to poke holes in my philosophy of the tool of violence and to find excuses for not confronting the uncomfortable truths I present to them.

"She must have had years of training," they say. *"She probably grew up with older brothers or something and knew how to handle herself."*

Of course, you know the truth. Sara has three younger sisters and almost no formal training, comparatively speaking. She hadn't trained in *any* capacity since our session on the cruise. Yet when faced with grievous bodily harm, her brain called up the situations we covered and the information she learned that day. *What do I know about this? How can I take care of myself? What can I do?* Her brain told her right away to be still—to remain calm. It told her that the only way to flip the odds in her favor was to wait until her attacker put himself in harm's way. As much as she hated the training while she was there, the basic principles of violence and self-protection had lodged in her brain. Over the three years between her training and her attack, they percolated and connected to her many real-world experiences, creating a deeper understanding of asocial violence, target identification, and the importance of inflicting injury. Her brain, *in the instant upon waking,* told her body what to do, and it saved her life.

AMMO-LESS + AIMLESS = USELESS

Sadly, not all the stories I've learned in my time as an instructor end like Sara's.

Joie Armstrong was a naturalist who worked for an educational partner of the National Park Service called the Yosemite Institute. As part of her job, she led nature hikes through Yosemite's backcountry teaching visitors about the area's ecology, topography, and geology. She knew the area and its people. In the summer of 1999, Joie was attacked outside her remote cabin on the edge of Yosemite National Park by a man named Cary Stayner, who restrained, abducted, and eventually murdered her.

It is a tragic, horrific story, but one that is not so simple for our purposes. From what the investigators described, when Stayner first encountered Joie alone outside her cabin, he pulled a gun and ordered her inside. When park police arrived, Joie's cabin was in shambles. Most of the furniture was broken, and various items had been strewn all over the floor. She put up a hell of a fight. She had scratched. She had clawed at him. But eventually he got hold of her, bound her hands together with duct tape, gagged her, put her into his truck, and drove into the woods.

Still, Joie did not stop fighting. She wrestled herself out of her bindings, jumped from the moving truck, and made a run for it. She got about 150 yards into the forest before Stayner caught up to her. By now he'd had enough. He drew a knife and slashed Joie's throat. Her body's instinctive response almost certainly stopped her in her tracks and drew her hands reflexively to the injury to her throat. That response sent adrenaline and increased blood flow to the site of the injury, only speeding up death. Any extra time she may have had was ruthlessly taken by Stayner who, in his homicidal rage, continued to cut at her neck until he'd decapitated her and threw her body into a nearby drainage ditch.

Joie was fit, independent, active. She was a skilled outdoorswoman with far more tenacity and physical strength than Sara. She was the opposite of Sara in nearly every meaningful way. But the major difference between the two young women—the one that really counted in the realm of unavoidable violence—was a brain trained with just a little bit of information. Trying to protect yourself from a psychopathic killer with an untrained brain, no matter how physically gifted you may be, is kind of like trying to fire an unloaded gun. You can kick and punch and scratch and claw—indeed, that is precisely what Joie did—but if your brain isn't loaded with the right information, it likely won't matter.

Joie had the capacity to be a larger caliber weapon with greater lethality, but tragically she had no bullets in her gun. A buoyant, life-loving personality whom her coworkers adored, Joie probably never thought about learning how to harness her power to inflict debilitating injury. Why would she? She takes kids on nature hikes for a living! Unfortunately, this effectively reduced her weapon to a bludgeon, one that she could only throw or swing wildly at her attacker. It is a painful reality to confront, but the limitations inherent in a lack of information and training probably cost Joie her life.

Sara's brain, by contrast, was fully loaded—with composure, with courage, with information, and with a plan. When Sara found herself in a life-or-death situation, with her perpetrator literally on top of her, the instinctive reactions of the unsuspecting mind—freezing, screaming, kicking, and punching wildly—were overridden by the learned actions of the trained mind. Sara unloaded her weapon, sending one through the eye and one through the throat, and it saved her life.

To extend this weaponized brain metaphor one last bit, I would be mistaken if I didn't talk about aim. Having the ammunition of information and training is critical. Understanding how to identify targets and being willing to pull the trigger is essential. But if you don't aim—or if your aim is bad—then none of it matters.

Aim, in this context, is the confidence and positivity of your self-talk. It's the *belief,* in your conscious mind, that you can call upon the principles of your training to solve whatever problem you face. When it comes to training your brain, whatever you tell yourself about your training, your abilities, your preparedness—it all inevitably comes true. If you tell yourself, *"In a life-or-death fight, I'm the equal of anyone who tries to attack me,"* that becomes true. If you tell yourself, *"I'm too small. I'm too weak. I'm not able to do this,"* your brain tells your body, *"Okay, we'll go with that."* And if you tell yourself nothing, then you're betting that your muscle memory and your unconscious understanding will be enough to save your life. Essentially, you're aiming into the darkness and firing with fingers crossed.

DON'T BE AFRAID OF FEAR

Through training your brain, you have the power to erase ignorance and reduce hesitation, but the one thing it cannot promise is the extinction of fear. Nor should it. Fear is a base, animal instinct. In any ecosystem, smaller, slower, weaker animals that live in the middle of the food chain have a very well-honed fear response. They can run fast, jump far, climb high, blend in well. And when their fear response is triggered, some combination of those physical attributes are engaged for the purpose of escape.

Fear has proven valuable to countless of these species across time the same way it has proven to be adaptive over 200,000 years of human evolution. It keeps us alive. Fear is our body's non-verbal warning signal of potential danger in our midst. In that sense, it is something we should try to tune into rather than try to silence.

This is true even for those people who have endured some of the most rigorous physical and mental training on earth. I am talking about the Special Operations soldier in the United States military. As a former Navy SEAL candidate, I can attest to the rigorous and relentless nature of both the physical and mental components of our training. It made us strong, fast, smart, and lethal. We became experts at using the tool of violence. What we did *not* become was robots.

When people talk about America's Special Operations Forces, you'll often hear words like "badass," "best of the best," "elite fighters," and "fearless warriors" tossed around. All those descriptions are true, except for one: *fearless.* Nearly every soldier, commando, law enforcement officer, and prison guard I have worked with is anything but fearless. To the contrary, they all have a healthy relationship with and respect for fear. They also stay far away from anyone who does not share those same feelings, because fearlessness is never far from recklessness. Fearlessness is what gets you trapped, outnumbered, outflanked, outgunned, and killed. Which is not to say that the fearful aren't brave or courageous, don't get me wrong. In fact, the opposite is true.

As Nelson Mandela famously said, "I learned that courage was not the absence of fear, but the triumph over it. The brave man is not he who does not feel afraid, but he who conquers that fear." But this is not a new opinion. Mandela is giving voice to Aristotle's ancient idea of the *golden mean*—the optimal, middle way between two extremes—as it relates to the virtue of courage.

I would add a caveat to that notion: the smart man is he who *listens* to that fear.

I often hear from clients who escaped or survived violent incidents only because they realized a situation was turning asocial *before* it escalated. Their brains had issued nonverbal warnings—*"Hey, something's wrong. You should get out of here."*—and they listened to them.

I hear from other clients who found themselves in inescapable asocial confrontations and reckoned with their fear as they leaned on their training to prevail and survive. Women like Sara and Bonnie. Men like Shawn and Peter. Tuning into their fear instead of ignoring or silencing it compelled them to respect the capabilities of their assailants and act quickly, smartly, and with the full force of their bodies. It gave them the awareness to understand, before it was too late, that they were in fights for their lives—and it gave them the burst of desperate energy it often takes to overcome hesitation, to act with intention, and to survive such a fight.

It is the kind of mental awareness that Mike, the bouncer at Jose Murphy's back in the 1980s, could have used before confronting the smaller, weaker man who surreptitiously pulled a knife and nearly bled him to death. Mike was never one to dismiss fear or pretend that he was never scared, but since he was surrounded by obvious physical threats all night, every night, his brain had started to lose the frequency for its warning signs. The skinny, squirrelly ex-con slumped over his beer on the barstool looked like the opposite of all the dangerous characters who any sane person was rightly afraid of, so Mike thought he was someone he didn't need to fear.

Conversely, I also hear about victims of violence who failed to remove themselves from dangerous situations in time, not because they lacked a sense of fear, but because they were more concerned with self-perception and social politics. They didn't want to seem paranoid, or to give offense. "I was suspicious, but I didn't want to be rude." "The guy looked strange but I couldn't figure out a nice way to leave." This kind of thing is more likely to happen in a larger public setting as opposed to isolated one-on-one encounters like

the ones most often described by my clients who escaped asocial confrontation.

The only kind of fear that holds no value for us is the
uncontrolled, unbounded, uninformed variety. Franklin Roosevelt summed up this notion perfectly in the most famous
sentence from his first inaugural address in 1933:

> So, first of all, let me assert my firm belief that the
> only thing we have to fear is fear itself—nameless,
> unreasoning, unjustified terror which paralyzes needed
> efforts to convert retreat into advance.

Everyone has heard the first half of that line, but has had
the most experience with the second. Clients like Bonnie
know that paralyzing terror in their bones, which is why the
second half of that FDR line is the most powerful to me.
Embracing fear in the face of life-or-death violence, without
the mental training we've covered in this section, only leads
to paralysis. And that's when people get killed. Mental training is not about overcoming or silencing fear, but about
learning how to channel fear into action. All you have to do
is listen to me, then listen to yourself.

DON'T WORRY, DESTRUCTION IS EASY

The difference between a violent criminal and an untrained
victim is that the violent criminal has prepared his brain to
go on the offensive. Violent criminals aren't often the sharp-
est tools in the shed, but in life-or-death confrontations, their
single-mindedness often works to their advantage. They know

that it is fundamentally simple to do real, catastrophic damage to a human body, so their mindset is constructed around that simple knowledge and the willingness to follow through on it. To neutralize that advantage and to capture the power of our own brains on offense—especially in moments of distress—we have to give it similarly simple commands, which is why I focus on principles. They're clear, straightforward, and they never change.

The important thing to remember is that training yourself to have an offensive mindset is not the same as training yourself to be a professional fighter. The execution of violence in a competitive environment implies an evenly matched opponent, a clear set of rules, and some kind of judge. None of those things are present, or relevant, when it comes to re-calibrating our brain for offense, or our goals once we do. And if they were, they would be completely useless to us, because competing against someone who's already been around the block a few times is very hard. It takes a lifetime to achieve the skill and proficiency of a professional martial artist, just as it does to become a master sculptor, for instance. It takes years of practice, precision, and patience. A novice sculptor couldn't carve Michelangelo's *David* or Rodin's *Thinker*. Fortunately, we're not trying to *build* anything here, per se. Our goal is destruction. If I said put down the chisel and forget the rules, then I gave you a sledgehammer, how long would it take you to figure out how to destroy that block of granite?

We've already seen how quick and easy it can be. Alex Gong spent his entire life chiseling his body and his mind in the image of a professional Muay Thai fighter, but it only took two reckless blasts from a stranger's handgun to shatter his life into a million pieces. My buddy Mike spent years learning how to handle himself as a bouncer and manage the toughest of tough-guy crowds, yet all it took was a couple quick swipes of a pocketknife from a guy half his size to fell him like a redwood tree.

In this way, the skillset for destruction is simple to acquire, and the mindset to execute is easy to achieve. That's all we really need to protect ourselves in life-or-death situations. This isn't about finesse or style points, after all. It's about mental readiness, about the willingness to seize the initiative, and about the confidence to channel fear and execute a plan under duress.

These are mental skills that *anyone* can master. The people I've discussed so far in this book are no different than you. A lot of them began with more baggage than you have right now, I bet. Think about Bonnie. I was extremely worried about her when she arrived at our training facility. She's not a violent person. She's not aggressive. She had experienced real violence before she began training, and she found our course emotionally and physically trying. We had to stop multiple times during the seminar so she could rebalance her feelings. But when she was practicing on the mats, she was getting the work done. And by doing the work, she was putting good information into her brain, priming her brain to act quickly and correctly if a critical moment ever came again. When the moment did come, in the Home Depot parking lot, her training probably saved her life. In a way, she was lucky to get that second chance. Most people don't survive the first.

When we look at stories of people like Bonnie and Sara and Shawn, and then contrast them with Joie's story, the difference becomes strikingly clear. What Bonnie and Sara and Shawn lacked in physical tenacity, they made up for with information. They didn't even have the opportunity to get away from their attackers. They didn't have the strength to beat their assailants in a fair fight. But they were able to protect themselves anyway, because they had trained their brains to recognize targets, to understand injury, and to aim for destruction.

The power of that combination—targets, injury, destruction—is also why teaching people like Bonnie and Sara and Shawn (or anyone, for that matter) how to execute intricate combat sequences is beside the point. Instead, we teach them about anatomy, and about the vulnerable parts of the human body, so that each of them had the confidence to injure their assailants and escape.

And yet I continue to run into men and women who—guided by misleading websites and under-educated instructors—insist on making things more complicated than they need to be. They're convinced that the confidence they need to protect themselves will come from mastering the best series of maneuvers and counterattacks for every conceivable situation. They want to memorize the entire multiplication table instead of learning how to multiply. They refuse to accept that protecting yourself isn't about "hitting here" or "punching there." They think that you can punch, jab, grab, kick, *or* stomp the neck to crush its cartilage (when the key concept is that damaged cartilage will lead to asphyxiation). They don't want to hear that the devil isn't actually in the details and that a specific set of moves is irrelevant if you don't understand the underlying principles of violence or *why* certain targets are better than others in *your unique situation.*

Without that knowledge, you won't have the confidence you need against a bigger, stronger, faster attacker. Without understanding anatomy, you may fall victim to the faulty assumption that hitting him in certain places—or not hitting him in others—will fail because he's so strong. Without the theory behind the strategies, or the target in front of the actions, your brain is more likely to give you commands that lock your human machine and, to reiterate the last phrase from President Roosevelt's famous line, paralyze the efforts needed to convert retreat into advance.

REALITY IS A BULLDOZER

Nobody wants to get hurt. If getting hurt were something that you could reliably choose to avoid, pain avoidance would be a central part of learning and training the tool of violence.

Unfortunately, it isn't.

The truth about violence is that you're going to get punched, kicked, stabbed, whacked, or shot, whether you're the "winner" or not. Any other outcome (e.g., you put your man, or men, down and keep them there without getting a scratch on you) is pure luck. What you can realistically expect as the survivor of an asocial confrontation is to limp out of there alive. Accepting the realities of violence like this ahead of time, and allowing your brain to process the fear that almost certainly comes with them, can save your life. It'll keep you from quitting right at the point where things are at their worst.

Remember Sergeant Young from the incident outside the Ukiah Walmart? He was a seventeen-year veteran and a well-trained martial artist versed in knife defense and standard law enforcement hand-to-hand combat scenarios. He effectively disarmed his knife-wielding attacker with a wrist-lock, but when he failed to see the man produce a gun with his other hand and then shoot him multiple times, his first thought wasn't, *Ohmygod I screwed up! Now I'm going to die!* He understood as part of his job and his training that eventually he was going to get hurt. He had accepted that reality. It allowed his brain to focus on survival and to issue simple commands to his body: call over the cadet, have him unholster your weapon, direct him to put it in your good hand, Fire! Fire! Fire!

Which thought do you want emerging from your brain when your life depends on it: "I'm done" or "Let's do this"? You're far more likely to find the latter thought coming out of you if you've accepted that there is no guaranteed, painless way out of unavoidable asocial violence—that survival is going to hurt.

What I'm describing is not some kind of transcendent feat of unbelievable heroism. This type of fortitude is not the exclusive domain of law enforcement officers or military personnel. Anyone can handle pain, including you. You are capable of more than you think. And the irony is, you don't have to change your relationship to pain in any other context but life-or-death violence. I bet Shawn and Peter have back pains from being on their feet all day as doctors. How much do you want to bet that Sergeant Young goes home at night, takes off his work boots, and complains about how sore they make his feet? None of those minor, ordinary pains disappeared. They're still the same people they were before; they'd just trained their brains to put all that aside and accept the reality of unavoidable, asocial confrontation when it finally reared up and hit them in the face. Adrenaline does a lot of the heavy lifting when it comes to enduring pain in the moment—when things are going fast and furious and your life is at stake, your brain doesn't have time for pain—but recognizing and accepting that pain is a big part of fighting off paralysis, and going immediately on the offensive.

This is a huge leap into uncomfortable places for most of you. For some, it might even feel a little masochistic. Rather than visualizing and training for violence the way we wished it worked, I am asking you to see it and train for it the way it is—to accept the pain. Believe me, it would be really nice if we could impose our collective will upon violent conflict—if waving our hands a certain way meant we couldn't be stabbed or shot. But that is magical thinking. Reality doesn't play by those imaginary rules. It is a smog-belching bulldozer with the elves and fairy-folk of nice ideals crushed by its iron treads.

The choice you have to make is whether you want to spend the rest of your life running from reality or putting yourself in its driver's seat. By training your brain to recognize the similarities in all humans rather than the differences, by understanding how to exploit those similarities when using the tool of violence has become unavoidable, and by learning how to act with the intent to injure completely, you are most definitely doing the latter and condemning your attacker to a short life doing the former.

If you choose to train the right way and imprint on your

brain what we have learned, I assure you, you will develop the confidence to face down any threat. I imagine all of this sounds easier said than done. The theories, principles, and strategies we've covered probably raise some questions: "How do I actually *do* this stuff? How do I train?" The answer, believe it or not, is right here in your hands.

CHAPTER EIGHT

TRAINING TIME

If effectiveness is doing the right things, efficiency is doing things right.

— *Tim Ferriss*

This is what the path to self-protection looks like when you step onto my mats, beginning on day one:

- We train anatomy to find targets
- We train with a plan to inflict injury
- We train with intention to bring full force
- We train slowly to be accurate and accustomed

Training is never more complicated than that, because violence is never more complicated than that. Whether in the hands of an asocial predator or an innocent civilian, to be effective, the tool of violence requires the same set of circumstances: the identification of a target somewhere on the body, to bring a strike with the full weight and intention of its user, to create debilitating injury. Always. Of course, you already knew that, because that's all we've talked about. To get started with your training and to actually do this stuff, begin by taking the lessons each featured scenario has taught us, and believe that you are capable of achieving the same kind of results that they achieved.

Think back to the Black Guerrilla Family members who identified gaps in the prison CERT team's new armor and slowly struck those areas on each other to perfect their aim. Recall the patience and the force Sara deployed on her attacker, or the opportunistic targeting by Shawn or Peter or Bonnie. They went for what they could get, with whatever they could use, giving it everything they had, to create injury. You can do that, too, right now. It really is that simple.

If you're anything like a former client of mine named David, however, you probably need to see the benefits of this slow, simple, deliberate philosophy in action to fully believe it. David didn't just get to *see* it, he got to *be* it one night in Tijuana.

Besides being a former client, David is also a great photographer who spent a good stretch of time in Tijuana a few years ago working on a documentary. In the 1980s, when I was in the Navy and living in San Diego, Tijuana was a relatively safe place to visit. On the weekends, it was full of teens from La Jolla and Los Angeles getting drunk in bars and then stumbling back across the border as the sun came up. Today, however, Tijuana is a different story. Since at least 2008, the Nueva Generacion and Sinaloa cartels have been fighting in the streets for control of the city, a major way station for narcotics trafficking up the I-5 corridor on America's west coast. As a result, murder has become a common, everyday occurrence.* Instances of brutal violence have become the rule, not the exception. It's gotten so bad in some areas of town that lesser acts of criminality get completely ignored, like car alarms in an average American city. Wander outside La Sexta (the touristy nightclub district) and violence can befall you in the blink of an eye.

One night, as David returned to his hotel, he heard a woman screaming. No one else on the street seemed to pay it any mind, but when the screams continued he ran, following the sound back behind the building, until he came upon two men dragging a girl into their car.

"Stop!" he yelled out.

They stopped, but only briefly. Without a word, one of the men left the girl with his partner as he ran up to challenge David, fists clenched and eyes dead. This was a textbook asocial situation, and David quickly recognized it as such. This guy was not closing the distance because he was excited about having a conversation — he was approaching with the explicit intent to cause an injury. David's brain quickly flipped through its rolodex of options.

He's bigger and probably stronger than me.
He's the one closing the distance.
He doesn't have a weapon, and neither do I.
His hands are down.
I can get the ear.

---

* In 2015, 670 people were killed in Tijuana alone; "New group fuels Tijuana's increased drug violence," *San Diego Union-Tribune*, February 13, 2016, www.sandiegouniontribune.com/news/border-baja-california/sdut-nueva-generacion-cartel-moves-tijuana-2016feb13-story.html.

In this split-second series of assessments, David made a calculation: he knew that if he could strike the man's ear correctly, he'd rupture the eardrum, opening the semicircular canal and emptying all the fluid (this is the same injury I suffered during my Navy SEAL training), which would induce vertigo and rip all sense of balance away from his opponent. It might not seem like a dramatic injury, but I can tell you from personal experience, it can be *immediately* disabling.

David stepped forward and open-palm slapped the man on the side of the head. The blow turned the man's head, exposing his neck, but only for a moment. The man turned back toward David and looked right through him, gritting his teeth. That was not the reaction David was hoping for.

Shit, it didn't work! David had executed what I call an "arm strike." He didn't move his body weight through the blow. He didn't use the tips we taught him, didn't try to put his belt buckle through the belt buckle of his attacker, dominating and overwhelming the man's center of gravity with his own. He struck him only with the weight his arm could generate, which is effectively a static strike with no kinetic force behind it.

I can imagine it was a bit like that cliché moment in movies where the action hero throws his best punch at the enormous Russian giant and it is simply absorbed with laughing indifference. It's funny when you're watching. It's terrifying if you're the one throwing the punch. I've seen it demoralize many a student as well. They think, *that was supposed to do something,* and when it doesn't, they freak out. They scramble.

Instead of panicking, David's brain kicked in with another automatic response: *You didn't step through. You need more force.*

Face to face with his potential assailant, David tried again, stepping through his target and applying his full body weight into the same move. This time, it was a textbook strike. This time, the guy went down on his ass. With no sense of balance or orientation, he was completely handicapped. When the man's partner saw his friend drop to the ground in a heap, he took off running, leaving the girl in the car and giving David ample time to get the girl out of there and call the authorities.

When David returned to the U.S., he told me his story and described how his training helped him to recover from his initial mistake. When his first attack failed, to his surprise, he didn't panic. In the past, he said, he probably would have fallen back on raw instinct, which would have told him to run. He would have wrongly bought into the perception that he was outmatched and destined to lose. But that instinct wasn't there this time—in its place was what he had practiced. He processed what he did wrong, corrected himself, and performed the move correctly the second time around. All in a matter of seconds—two slaps, *bam bam*— that's all it took.

I asked David what he thought it was about our training that made the difference. He said he wasn't sure, but I knew. The key was training *slow.*

In my seminars, we deliberately train in slow motion—way slower than the speed of a real fight, or even traditional sparring that you'd find in an MMA gym or a boxing ring. And David, like many students, had challenged me on that. He said, "A real fight happens at full speed. Why aren't we learning how to do everything quickly? How am I supposed to react fast enough if we only train slow?" David's concerns sound intuitive enough, but what we need to recognize is that learning speed isn't something we need to invest that time in.

Why? Because speed takes care of itself. We're wired for speed (and strength). If I took you into a boxing gym and stuck you in front of a heavy bag and told you to punch and kick it as fast and as hard as you could, you can do that. What you *can't* do is reliably hit specific targets as fast or as hard. Watch the average public speaker. Rarely do you find yourself saying: this guy is going way too slow, pick it up. It's far more common that they rush through their talk, carried as they were on nervousness and insecurity. My first talk, which I had repeatedly practiced and padded so I would hit my allotted thirty minutes, went well. Then I looked at the clock—I'd somehow shaved nearly ten minutes off in front of the audience.

In a life-or-death moment, the instinctual fear response and the resulting adrenaline and norepinephrine rushes propel nearly all your critical body functions: heart rate, lung capacity, pupil dilation, fast-twitch muscle response, energy distribution from glucose stores. They all speed up in pace or increase in volume. Essentially, quickness comes automatically.

What will *not* come automatically is a command of the principles and techniques you need to save your life. Those you need to etch into your brain. In my experience, that's only something a slow training tempo can provide: it allows you to internalize the movements and commit them to memory. Even when you're afraid, even when your conscious mind feels blank, those moves remain stored in your muscle memory, ready to activate when you need them. With enough practice at the right pace, your muscles will remember how to perform the right actions, even if your conscious mind needs a little time to catch up.*

A PLAN OF ACTION

Training slow also helps you develop a plan. Everyone needs a plan. Not a step-by-step, punch-here-kick-here kind of plan, as we discussed in the last chapter. Those are unrealistic and fantastical. What you need is a set of general rules—*fundamentals,* really—that you will engage and follow if you find yourself in an inescapable confrontation.

Nowhere have I seen this principle more effectively demonstrated than by the La Nuestra Familia gang at another of California's maximum-security detention centers. I was visiting this prison to meet with corrections officers and discuss the key differences in training for contact out in the yard versus contact in confined spaces. As we got to talking, one of the ranking officers told me about the recent assassination of a Nuestra shotcaller.†

This guy had been instructing his crew to produce and sell adulterated drug product to the Aryans in the prison and it was causing problems both in the prison and out in the streets. The leaders of La Nuestra Familia outside of the

---

* Interestingly, it's the combination of these mental processes and physical practices that is responsible for the sensation of time slowing down in high-stakes, high-stress moments like a fight for your life.

† In prison, a shotcaller is the leader of a gang who makes decisions about the duties, ranks, and punishments of its imprisoned members. Sometimes he is even powerful enough to dictate what happens out on the streets.

prison finally decided they'd had enough and they ordered this shotcaller's lieutenants to take him out. But to pull this off, they needed a plan. In a prison under constant video and human surveillance, you can't just attack someone and expect to both be successful and get away with it. The lieutenants decided they would take out their shotcaller on the basketball court.

You'd think out in the open in the yard would be the last place anyone would want to stage a high-profile execution, but these guys knew what they were doing. The shotcaller loved playing basketball in the yard. He'd play almost every day. That meant that the guards on duty in the towers wouldn't think twice about seeing him out there on the court surrounded by his guys. It would look like business as usual and they could focus more of their attention on other areas of the yard. Additionally, basketball would get the shotcaller's heart rate elevated, which would increase the speed with which he bled out if they were successful.

The rest of the plan was simple: they would play with him every day for a couple weeks. In each game, whoever was on his team would purposefully set him up for easy drives to the basket or open looks for jump shots. Whenever he made a shot, his teammates would casually come over from all sides and congratulate him. They'd smack him in his shirtless belly, pat him on the back of the neck, wrap him around the waist in a mini-hug, pound his chest enthusiastically like they were psyched up about winning. To both the shotcaller and the guards on duty, these gestures appeared like run-of-the-mill ring-kissing by lower-level guys to their boss. And by doing it day after day for a couple weeks, it became an unremarkable piece of the scenery.

What the guards and the shotcaller didn't realize was that each of those congratulatory gestures was aimed at a specific vulnerable area on the human body. The smacks on the belly dialed in a stab to the gut and the liver. The pat on the neck homed in on the carotid artery. The waist grab found the spleen and the bottom of the rib cage. The chest punch zeroed in the heart, the lungs, and the nerve running from the neck down the shoulder. The lieutenants were getting the shotcaller used to being touched in these vulnerable target areas so when the assassin made his move, first contact would not be so difficult, which would make the second strike less difficult, and so on down the line until the shotcaller was on the ground.

When the day finally arrived, everyone played basketball as usual. The assassin slipped onto the court inside what became a ring of guys—all of whom the shotcaller trusted—who shielded the attack from view. The assassin struck nearly every body part the lieutenants had softened up for him with ruthless, deliberate precision. The whole thing took less than five seconds. The lieutenants slowly dispersed, like they did every time the game was over. By the time guards finally realized something was wrong on the basketball court, the shotcaller had bled out. When medical assistance finally arrived, he was already dead.

What I have just described might seem at first like an elaborate plan, but in reality, it was very simple. It came down to this:

1. We have one shot at this.
2. Identify the vulnerable targets.
3. Give it everything you've got for five seconds.

Now, morally and legally speaking, training to be a murderous predator is worlds away from training to *protect* yourself from a murderous predator, but in either case a basic nuts-and-bolts plan for dealing with life-or-death violence is essential to getting through it. Once you have developed and learned that plan, it's critical that you walk through it until it's second nature and you have the confidence to execute it with proper form, force, and accuracy. Rehearsing the assassination of their shotcaller for two weeks seared the plan into the brains of the Nuestra lieutenants and it allowed the assassin to perform with precision when it was time to act.

Despite his skepticism about training slowly, I think David understood this concept very well. His initial failure, after all, was not one of ignorance (no plan) or arrogance (no *need* for a plan). He had a plan for his kind of situation, one he'd practiced on the mats several times before. His training had ingrained the correct move and the proper form into his muscle memory, so that if the time to act at full speed ever came, he'd be ready. David's mistake was that he went *too fast*, landing a blow in the right spot, at the right time, just with the wrong amount of force behind it. He didn't give himself that split second he needed to load up and transfer all his body weight into the strike and through his attacker. Once he recognized his error, he simply had to re-engage his plan. He acted without hesitation and mere seconds after the insufficient initial delivery, the fight-ending blow found its mark.

Having this plan, practicing it, and training it the right way is so vital, no matter how unlikely it is that asocial violence will find you. It's why schools conduct earthquake and fire drills by having their students crawl under their desks or move in an orderly fashion down the nearest stairwell and through the nearest exit. Going through the motions makes them readier for the real thing, which can be the difference between life and death. It certainly was for David.

SLOW IS SMOOTH, SMOOTH IS FAST, FAST IS DEADLY

Inflicting injury is all about the fundamentals. The same is true of pretty much any skill. We learn complicated ideas and actions by breaking them down into their most basic elements and mastering those elements in turn, whether we're learning to hit a baseball or play a piano.

When it comes to self-defense, I've found that this crucial aspect of training is missing from nearly everyone's curriculum, and to me, that's a huge mistake: slowness, deliberateness, mastery of fundamentals — they're the foundation on which everything else is built. Without form, force, *and* accuracy, you won't generate the effect you want. And if you move too quickly in your training, all those things suffer. In fact, errors will start to compound themselves. If you have bad form, speed will make the situation worse. You'll be off balance, which leads to poor accuracy, which leads to a lack of force. You'll be like David in his first, failed attempt to neutralize his attackers. Just a slight inadequacy of force was the difference between a potentially crippling blow and awkwardly slapping someone upside the head.

Jam your thumb in someone's eye, like Sara did, and you blind the person and produce sympathetic tearing in the other eye, so that what vision remains is out of focus. Miss by an inch, however, and you've created a bruised and pissed off assailant. Had Shawn practiced slips and trips at speed instead of one step at a time, when he went to yank out his attacker's leg under the car door there could have been a very real possibility that he moved too fast and only pulled the man's shoe off; leaving him mobile enough on one leg to reach over the car door and empty a magazine into Shawn, who would have been prone on the ground with nowhere to go.

When you're training to protect yourself and others, speed always comes last. In the more than twenty-five years I've been training people in self-protection, I've never heard from someone who used self-protection tools in the field and felt like they suffered from a lack of speed at the moment of truth. In fact, I usually hear the opposite: it's much more common to suffer from a lack of accuracy or force.

Remember, this is real-life violence, not a kung-fu movie or a competition. Your goal isn't to trade lightning-fast blows with your opponent until you work him into a corner. Your goal is to inflict a decisive, debilitating injury to the best target you can find. The more you rush your training, the more likely you are to miss your target or deliver an ineffective blow. Fifteen decent hits in rapid succession is great for scoring points in an Olympic tae kwon do match, but unless you're able to deliver that one devastating strike to a vulnerable area, it's not very useful two-on-one in an alley behind a Mexican border town hotel.

If you prioritize speed, not only will the results be terrible, but you'll create a negative feedback loop where those terrible results convince you that you're still too slow—so maybe you'll take the wrong lesson and speed up even more, which will further cement bad habits and poor performance.

How To Safely Train To Deliver Injuries

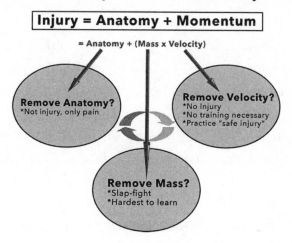

Injury = Anatomy + Momentum

= Anatomy + (Mass x Velocity)

Remove Anatomy?
*Not injury, only pain

Remove Velocity?
*No Injury
*No training necessary
*Practice "safe injury"

Remove Mass?
*Slap-fight
*Hardest to learn

This is not a sustainable path to mastery of *anything*, because it makes it impossible to learn from your mistakes.

That's why I don't want you thinking you are Jackie Chan. I don't need you at the gym rapid-fire attacking the heavy bag like your goal is Roy Jones Jr.–level hand speed. If you are ever in a fight for your life it is never going to look like Mike Tyson landing a five-punch combination in six seconds. More likely, we will be talking about one or two blows, at most. Think back to the fights in this book:

Sara used an eye gouge and a throat strike.
Mike the bouncer went down from two nearly invisible
    knife wounds.
Bonnie used a throat strike and a knee stomp.
Shawn used a knee drop and an ankle joint break.
Peter used his forearm to smash the radial nerve then
    strike the throat.

David, on his second try, effectively used a palm strike to the ear.

That is six potentially do-or-die fights ended by injury in twelve combined strikes. That's two per incident. Excepting David's first strike, which he learned from, each one was delivered at the right time, in the right place, with the correct amount of force to weaken and then immobilize an attacker. If you train those moves too fast, however, you'll almost certainly make so many errors that you can't possibly be aware of them all, and when it finally counts, you're likely to miss, or strike with insufficient force to cause the injury you absolutely need. Training fast is training haphazardly, which is to train for chaos instead of control.

What you really want is to go slowly and smoothly to get everything exactly right. One square inch of you through one square inch of him. Visualize your mass driving whatever tool you have—a stick, a knife, your boot, your fist—three feet through him, trying to make it come out the other side. Visualize displacing him and standing where he once stood. Your belt buckle through his belt buckle. Then go and do it.

You also want to be acutely, embarrassingly aware of every mistake you make—missing the target, using an improperly configured tool (like a loose fist), losing your balance. You want these errors to pop up one at a time so you can register them individually and adjust yourself to each specific problem to correct them. This trains your brain to do exactly what you want, the way you want it, even when you add speed to the equation later.

Fundamentally, the slower you practice, the smoother

your actions become, the closer to mastery you get. For the purposes of training the tool of violence, mastery is a three-factor test. If any one of them fails, mastery has not been achieved and the training in that area should be slowed down.

1. You get everything you want exactly right.

Practicing violence is training for survival. When you're in a fight for your life, you never want to do something that you've "sort of" worked on or gotten good at "more or less." Everything you go for, you want to get exactly right. That means if you miss it in training, slow down. If your mass wasn't fully involved, slow down. If the strike, joint break, or throw didn't work the way you intended, slow down. Adjust the pace of your training to make your practice perfect.

2. You are always in balance.

A professional baseball player in balance can hit a 95-mile-per-hour fastball 450 feet with what seems like very little effort. When he gets out on his front foot, though, he ends up reaching out and flailing at the pitch, often popping the ball up weakly on the infield. If he hesitates and is stuck on his back foot, he gets handcuffed and struggles even to make contact.

The same principle applies in violence when you are being attacked and forced to defend yourself. When you're in balance you control where your mass goes and you can swing it like a sledgehammer. When you're off balance, you've lost control of your weapon and reduced its power exponentially, and now *you* are the vulnerable one. Your center of gravity is compromised. You're too far out over your skis, as the saying goes. Go as fast as you want, as long as your balance is constant and absolute. If it's not—slow down.

3. Your partner can give you clean, clear reactions.

In a real fight, every injury you inflict changes the shape of the human machine into a new configuration of targets and balance. You need to see those reactions in your practice, too, so you can be ready to respond to them in real life. Learning those reactions allows you to use injury tactically and to fight in rhythm, predicting when and where new targets will appear based on the injury just inflicted. From Shawn's training on the mats, for instance, he knew that once he smashed the bones in the top of his attacker's foot, it would open access to the heel, ankle joint, and lower leg. He also knew that if his attacker had been kneeling instead of standing when Shawn leveled the knee drop, the subsequent target would have presented differently, which would have required a different approach to the injury that finally incapacitated the attacker.

The human response to particular types of trauma is predictable, but also specific to the position of the victim's body (standing, kneeling, bent over, on all fours, prone) in relation to the position of the attacker's body and the angle of attack. If you go faster than your partner's ability to give you those clean, predictable reactions, you'll cloud your training with a bunch of useless noise. In plain English, if it feels to your partner like you are bolting around the training mats like a wild person, your partner's instinct is going to be to cover up and fend off your assault, instead of simulate the predictable human response to the injury you're training to inflict. That is helpful to no one, because life-or-death violence shouldn't feel like a manic slap-fight to either member of a training duo.*

This can be frustrating if your coordination is more advanced than your training partner's and you can do things like hit the same number of targets with fewer strikes, in fewer moves. That kind of advanced coordination makes you want to go, go, go. You can have perfect targeting and the balance of an Olympic gymnast, but your rate of speed will always be governed by your partner's ability. An expert working with a new student will still have to slow down, for example. But it's important to realize that the goal of training is not simply to turn *you* into a badass. It's to slowly increase *both* partners' understanding and abilities.

Once you've mastered those three criteria, you can gradually add in speed. Not that you need to. The person with the most real-world experience with asocial violence in my cadre of instructors (by virtue of his job history) trains slower than everyone and has never changed. Students and other instructors call him Instructor Molasses, but he doesn't care. He tells new people right away: "Hey, I train slow. You want to train faster, train with somebody else." Working successfully at speed can be achieved faster than most people would believe, just ask Instructor Molasses, but only if you take the slow road to mastery.

---

* One of the criteria to judge self-protection instructors and their training facilities by is the quality of the other students and their ability to partner you up appropriately.

YOU NEVER OUTGROW THE BASICS

My slow-paced, fundamental-centric training philosophy is somewhat unique to self-protection and the tool of violence, but it is practically traditional when it comes to the acquisition and mastery of a difficult skill.

Look at firearms training. If you have a good instructor, you'll first learn how to dry fire without any bullets. You'll learn all the fundamentals of holding and aiming a gun. After you've internalized that information, you'll dry fire at a stationary target, learning how to pull the trigger with as little jerk and lift as possible. Then you'll learn how to load the weapon. Next, you'll start shooting with live ammunition, usually one round at a time in single-shot groups. You'll slowly and deliberately try to hit your target, repeatedly. Then you'll move on to multiple-shot groups, where you fire a quick succession of shots at the target. Once your aim is consistently good (which could take days or weeks), your instructor might introduce the concept of a moving target. If you maintain accurate targeting in that phase, the instructor will introduce the next phase—which is hitting a moving target while *you're* also moving.

At any stage of the game, if there's a failure or regression of any kind—if you start to lose your targeting capacity and your shot groupings start to widen—you'll default back to the slow, deliberate targeting of a sedentary target. This is how skilled instructors train beginners in the basics, but it's also how the best in the business stay sharp. The system never changes: break everything down to fundamentals. Repeat, repeat, repeat. When you can perform those fundamentals in your sleep, you'll know you've mastered them.

When I was interviewing law enforcement officers in Los Angeles about prison gangs for this book, a Los Angeles County Sheriff's Department sergeant told me about a recent firearms training session his team went through at one of the department's shooting ranges.

The session was being taught by a highly trained operator from the Army's Delta Force unit. The sergeant was assigned to help set up the range and get the course ready before the other officers arrived. An early riser, the sergeant got there at six-thirty a.m., well ahead of the ten o'clock start time—but not ahead of the Delta operator. He was already there, waiting to do a walk-through and a practice run of his own to familiarize himself with the course.

The sergeant quickly opened the range and watched the Delta operator get to work. During the first hour, the operator slowly and dynamically drew his weapon and dry-fired from a variety of positions. In the second hour, he started adding ammo and shooting moving targets. He practiced slowly and deliberately, making sure all his shots were on the mark. During the third hour, he started moving around and shooting with various weapons systems—periodically defaulting back to the slower movements to make sure his form was crisp. When the training session finally began at ten, the operator demonstrated the course at full speed. Flawlessly.

"If I hadn't opened the range that day, I would have thought this guy was superhuman and had amazing natural skills," the sergeant told me as he finished his story. "I would never have seen all the slow, deliberate work that allowed him to perform at a high level."

The Delta operator used his three-hour warm-up to make small corrections, then he translated those tweaks into fast, accurate execution during the actual course. This was a special forces operator, remember. Active duty or retired, he would easily rank among the top 1 percent in the world when it comes to handling a firearm. In his career, he has probably aimed and fired hundreds of thousands of rounds. And yet, when it came time to prepare for a moment that counted—or honestly, even a moment that didn't really count, since he was just teaching a class—he went right back to the same drills that beginners practice the first time they pick up a gun. He did them one at a time, and he went through them slowly. He hadn't outgrown the basics of his training, and he probably never will.

It turns out the best of the best in *any* discipline work this way. That deep practice, built on slow, excruciating repetition, focused on accuracy and correctness, is what separates the elite from the also-ran. This is especially true for disciplines that require fast execution. My friend Daniel Coyle wrote a book called *The Talent Code* that examined the tools and habits of experts in fields as diverse as sports, music, math, and science, among others. Across the board, they all used the same process: slow training, deep practice, fast execution.

One of the interesting stories in *The Talent Code* involves a music academy with a seemingly odd rule. If a teacher walked by a practicing violin student and they could recognize what was being played, that meant the student was playing too fast. Each stroke had to be excruciatingly slow, because what they were asking students to work on wasn't perfecting particular pieces, but rather ingraining the habits of perfect form with the bow and fingers, understanding that it was much easier to speed up habits learned slowly than to correct for bad form learned too fast.

It was like they were taking a page right out of the book of the famous violinist and orchestra conductor, Joseph Bologne, Chevalier de Saint-Georges, but not for the reasons you'd suspect. Born in the French West Indies in the second half of the eighteenth century, Saint-Georges was also known for being a duelist and champion fencer.

Early in his career, while other fencers practiced fast footwork, elaborate strikes, and clever distraction techniques, Saint-Georges spent most of his time going through a peculiar training routine. He would draw three dots on the wall and spend an inordinate amount of time slowly and deliberately poking each dot with his sword. He'd step in, and thrust. Step in, and thrust. Over and over again.* It was a regimen that earned him continual mockery from people who had never seen him duel. When they did, the mockery disappeared.

In duel after duel, Saint-Georges would dispatch his opponents with uncanny accuracy and lightning-fast efficiency. He was so good, so accurate, so *effective,* that even in social situations it was said that he could flick the buttons off the shirt of any man within his sword's reach. It was an incredible feat—not only of dexterity, but of consistency—and one for which he was given the nickname, "The Button Man."

Saint-Georges understood the importance of precision. With most his time spent on just three simple targets, Saint-Georges certainly wasn't having as much fun as his rivals. His had to be the most tedious, most basic training technique of any of them. It was also the most effective.

---

* This is not unlike the prison inmates from Chapter Five, who practiced stabbing vulnerable areas on a prison guard's body using broomsticks and chalk outlines on their cell walls.

Perfecting the basics of a difficult skill through deep, slow practice doesn't just increase your effectiveness and efficiency with that skill, it has the benefit of being safer as well. My friend Tony is a professional dancer and a very skilled roller skater. He was a cast member in Andrew Lloyd Webber's Broadway show, *Starlight Express*. It was a play performed completely on roller skates at blindingly fast speeds. Any deviation from the choreography by a performer could be devastating to the whole ensemble and bring a performance to a screeching halt. One wrong move could cause a chain-reaction of collisions and injuries.

Everyone in the *Starlight Express* cast was a top-rated dance talent. They could all do challenging moves with ease—on roller skates, no less! Yet, for the first six weeks of rehearsal, they slowly and deliberately walked through every single movement on carpet, on foot, so they could get it exactly right. Until they had the routines memorized, until they could perform the entire show at walking speed on a padded surface, they never even put on a skate. When they finally strapped on their skates, they still weren't ready to perform at full speed. They started again with slow and deliberate movements through each routine. They weren't allowed to add velocity until every sequence was perfect.

Sound familiar? This is precisely how firearms training progresses. It's how I construct my self-protection training methods. And it just so happens to be the safest way to do either of them. When Tony finished describing his time in *Starlight Express*, he told me, "Our whole group was injury-free through the entire run of the show, which *never* happens."

Firearms, music, fencing, roller skating, violence: no matter the discipline, the lesson is the same. If you *train slow*, you never outgrow the basics, because the training hardwires them into your instincts while simultaneously taking conscious thought out of the equation for when you need to operate in a hurry.

In the context of violence, it might sound something like this: *"Okay, If I'm trying to crush the throat, I want my foot to be placed here when I deliver the blow. I want to step through and use my ulna bone [pinky side of forearm]. I want to step all the way through the individual so I end up standing where he used to be. And I want to make sure I have good, solid structure as I strike the throat."*

If you move slowly enough through the moves during your training, you can literally talk yourself through each component, giving your brain time to process the information without missing anything. You also get to deliberately touch and push through target areas, which delivers huge kinesthetic learnings on top of the auditory and visual methodologies that are standard to all forms of deep practice. Then when it's time to perform in the real world, the data is intact, the muscle memory is engaged, and in the heat of the moment, speed takes care of itself.

THE SEESAW EFFECT: HOW SPEED KILLS

One of the more popular, exciting buzzwords in our world today is *scenario-based training*. In this fast-paced training modality, an instructor will mock up a specific real-world scenario, then explain how to deal with it in a series of defined, exacting steps. The context and directions are always very clear.

I'm going to the ATM.
I get approached from behind on my left side.
He places his right hand on my neck.
I'm going to do move 1.
Then I'm going to do move 2.
And finally, I will do move 3.
I've just cleared the threat.

Boom, boom, boom. One, two, three. Easy, right? As you probably figured by now, it's never that simple. If there's one thing I've learned from my time in the Navy, and working with elite fighting units, law enforcement officers, and prison guards, it's that real violence never happens the way you expect. You can watch ten thousand hours of violence videos and no two incidents will be alike. In that way, training for specific scenarios is banking your training on the hope that those precise scenarios are the ones that arise when your life is on the line—which is about as likely as winning the lottery. You're better off instead focusing on preparedness, trying to identify what most violent incidents have in common, and training to exploit or protect yourself against those commonalities.

Of course, fast, scenario-based training might teach you a series of three moves to execute when someone approaches you from the left and puts their right hand on your neck, but it won't teach you how to handle yourself when that guy shifts to your right side, or his buddy shows up, or he's shorter than you, or he's wearing gloves that are hard to grab, or he hits you with the butt of his gun.

Oddly, we seem to be okay with the philosophy behind this style of self-defense training, even though if you were to use those techniques to train one of the other skills we just talked about, like firearms training, it would immediately appear ridiculous. Imagine that a firearms instructor shows you how to turn off your gun's safety, then says, "There are five guys on the other side of this door arrayed in front of you from three o'clock to nine o'clock. They all have guns. When I push you through the door, they're going to start shooting and I want you to execute the three moves we just covered. Good luck."

It does not take a genius to recognize how ridiculous that would be. What if the guy at nine o'clock drops behind a table and maneuvers to your seven o'clock, drawing your attention away from the guy at one o'clock who just decided to close the distance on you? What if there were only two guys all along, and in the time it took you to register that the threat was actually smaller than you thought, they'd each put three bullets in your chest?

A bullet is just as lethal as a violent predator who has targeted you, so why does this kind of fast, scenario-based training seem ludicrous with firearms, but completely fine with self-defense? What, exactly, is the fascination with creating an imaginary attack scenario?

Honestly, I think it's because it's fun. Because it gives students an easy (yet false) sense of security, and because it lets them play-act fights in a safe environment. They can live out those intruder and active shooter fantasies that have occupied their imaginations late at night waiting to fall asleep. It's the kind of training that sells because it's user-friendly, but that doesn't mean it works. Put more bluntly, that kind of training can get you killed, because training at full speed creates a seesaw effect: speed goes up, accuracy and force go down, the likelihood of inflicting injury trends toward zero on the street, but goes up on the mats.

Think of it this way. Go back to the three major requirements for inflicting injury:

1. A target: a vulnerable piece of anatomy on the other person.
2. A weapon: a sturdy piece of your own anatomy to make contact with the vulnerable piece on your opponent.
3. Force: You need to strike with your full body weight, which means you need to step through the action.

To do all of this, you need to be accurate. We're targeting areas of the body that cause life-threatening injuries here. These areas aren't big flashing targets with massive bull's-eyes (evolution wouldn't allow that). You can't just hit an assailant in the face. You have to target a very specific area on the face, like the eye or the ear, and strike it with your full body weight.

If you train too quickly, however, you will have a tendency to strike too fast, which inevitably forces you to sacrifice accuracy. If you lose accuracy, you end up hitting ineffective areas on the human body. You may cause nonspecific trauma, but that's just pain (as opposed to injury), which means your enemy can gut it out and fight back. When he keeps coming, you panic, because your first attack failed. You attack even more quickly and haphazardly, with even less accuracy. Soon, you're flailing wildly, ineffectively, fatally. That's the worst-case scenario in a life-or-death situation. And it's likely to happen for those who haven't practiced the fundamentals of violence enough to make them part of their muscle memory.

This is precisely what slow training is designed to do: to inculcate foundational principles and ensure you absorb them as "deep practice" into your unconscious mind and your muscle memory so you can handle any scenario that comes your way. Repeating a move in slow motion, again and again, isn't nearly as fun as wailing on a punching bag or dive rolling into a room after a door breach. I admit that— but I don't want you to have fun: fun is fatal. The point of this training isn't entertainment, it's effectiveness. And to effectively inflict injury, you can't sacrifice accuracy, and you can't sacrifice force. You can only sacrifice speed. By dialing back training tempo as much as 90 percent, you increase your capacity for mastering the mental and physical tools of self-protection, and you build the kind of confidence that comes from knowing you can tackle any situation.

There's no other way to put it: slow practice is deep practice, and deep practice leads to mastery.

CHAPTER NINE

TRAINING TO INFLICT INJURY

Pain don't hurt.

—Road House, 1989

Violence begins and ends with injury. Injury is its raison d'être. In a fight for your life, there is no substitute for inflicting injury on your enemy. It is, in no uncertain terms, the arbiter of success in violence. Those who fully understand this have a distinct advantage over those whose understanding is dim and instinctual. That's why I teach these principles to everyone who comes through my doors and why I have made some version of this point multiple times already in this book: I want to sear the knowledge, and the advantage, into your brain for all time.

When you're left without a choice, act first, act fast, aim for a target, and give it everything you've got until your attacker is incapacitated and you're standing where he once stood. Injury, injury, injury.

Injury changes everything in your favor. In violent conflict, injury is the portal through which you get to pass into the rest of your life. When things go bad—let's say your attacker pulls a gun—your options narrow to a single question: "Act or hope?" If he shoots you dead, it's over. But if you get a thumb into his eye, like Sara did to her attempted rapist, and he falls to the ground with debilitating, agonizing trauma, it's the key opening the lock to the rest of your days.

But how do you know if you've actually injured someone and that door to your future has been unlocked? How can you be sure you did it right—accurately, with proper form and enough force? For the purposes of determining effective violence, injury has three primary criteria: it is objective, it is decremental, and it is lasting.

Injury is objective. When an injury has occurred, all disinterested third parties can agree. A broken leg is obvious from across the street—someone crumpling to the ground holding a limb bending sharply in an unnatural direction is hard to miss. Someone clutching their throat gasping for air is unmistakable. The stunned look of someone who has just had their own knife turned around and plunged into their chest is impossible to forget. Moreover, as we've already covered, injured people move in predictable ways. The body responds to injury through the somatic reflex arc— the spinal reflex reactions I talked about earlier. These are pre-programmed, specific movements, triggered by a large stimulus (like crushed testicles). The threshold switch that decides whether to trigger the reflex is in the spinal cord, not the brain. Thus, there is no conscious choice involved, just physics and physiology.

These reflexes are injury-specific, meaning that a boot to the groin elicits the same basic response in all humans. A man you've kicked in the groin will bend his knees and double over with his chin up—*whether he wants to or not.* This means it is very difficult for your opponent to hide his injury from you, or from anyone who knows what they're looking at. And since you can already predict from your training how your enemy will move when you injure him in a specific way, you have a knowledge base against which to verify his reaction and, ideally, take full advantage of it.

Injury decrements body function. Injury alters the normal functioning of the body in a negative, unavoidable way. A broken leg just plain doesn't work. It may, in fact, prevent the entire body it's connected to from working. This is the key distinction that separates pain from injury. Pain can slow function, but that effect is relative since different people have different pain thresholds. For some a torn fingernail is agony, for others a torn-off finger goes unnoticed. That's because much of our response to pain originates from the brain once the nerve endings at the site of trauma make their way up through the dorsal horn of the spinal cord.

Injury, by comparison, takes the brain completely out of play. The concussive force at the site of trauma sends shock waves through the nervous system that slam into the dorsal horn, creating an automatic reflex response before the brain has even been able to register what happened. The equation is simple: Excessive force plus a vulnerable anatomical target equals injury. This has nothing to do with pain or the psychological state of the recipient. Even for the person who can ignore a ripped-off finger, there's nothing his brain can do about his physical inability to pull a trigger or press a button with that finger. It's just not going to work.

This is true for any injury that eliminates his ability to function, no matter how great his physical and psychological advantages were before the trauma. Is he stronger than you? Not with a crushed throat, he isn't. Is he faster than you? Not with a shattered knee. Is he far more dangerous than you, with scads of training, experience, a gun, and an indomitable iron will? Not with a broken neck.

Injury is lasting. Injury lasts for the whole course of the encounter, and beyond. It requires medical attention to heal. If your leg is broken, you can't "rub some dirt on it" and then expect to "walk it off." You can't walk *at all.* All true injuries open the same opportunity: to take advantage of a degraded opponent in the throes of a spinal reflex reaction who has been rendered helpless against being injured again and again.

I'm sure that sounds a little dark, but just remember, in a fight for one's life, fairness is out the window. Anything we do that does not cause an injury is worthless to us. Every time we touch him, we need to break something inside him. Every time we touch him, we need to make a part of him cease normal function. Injure him, drop him, and keep on injuring him until he's nonfunctional. We're not done until we're sure he's done. And the way to be sure is if he very obviously cannot function and won't be able to for some time (if ever). That's how we know we've done our job.

The rest of this chapter is dedicated to the principles behind the three fundamental methods for causing injury. Three mechanisms for taking all that knowledge now etched into your brain and transferring it through your body into the vulnerable areas of a violent predator who attacks you.

They are: striking, joint-breaking, and throwing.

Striking is the most basic way to inflict injury: throwing your entire mass through a single target to wreck it. It forms the basis for all violence; every method by which to deliver injury will derive its power from striking. Striking is what drives the knife deep into the body and opens the skull with a blow from a baton. It's how injury gets done.

Joint-breaking is applying the principles of striking to vulnerable joints. It is not a joint-lock aimed at compliance or submission — the way that martial arts bouts usually end — since those don't have permanent injury as a goal or outcome. Breaking a joint is about blasting past the pathological limit of that joint to destroy the connective tissue so it doesn't work anymore.

Throwing is applying a strike to get people airborne and power them into the ground. It allows you to do things you can't do with your bare hands — like fracture his skull. Throwing is just another way to cause injury; it's beating the man with the planet.

These are the things you need to know how to do when you are training for injury.

STRIKING 101

Striking is about tearing, rupturing, and shattering. Striking is about wreckage. The goal of striking is to impart the largest possible load of kinetic energy (kE) into your target to achieve that state of injury and disrepair. The most obvious examples of striking are kicking and punching. Yet the number-one fallacy regarding striking is that it has to be done solely with the arms and legs. This misconception leads to a loss of focus and proper perspective — the punch or kick is immaterial; it's never about the fist or foot. It's all about the broken ribs.

When we think of striking as something done with the limbs alone, we enter a negative feedback loop that keeps us from achieving the goal of violence, because our arms and legs are not able to generate the kinetic energy required to cause debilitating injury, without fail, every time. Even worse, untrained students often hold back and snap off their punches and kicks, failing to follow through — a defensive instinct that may temporarily prevent your opponent from grabbing hold of you, but also reduces the likelihood of causing useful injury to him — which of course just makes you that much more reluctant to commit to any one punch or kick. Then targeting goes out the window. There is even less follow-through now. He remains uninjured. And so it goes until someone gets tired of getting slapped around and quits, either by capitulating, disengaging, or pulling a gun and escalating the scenario.

Thinking "I'm punching now" puts you on the wrong side of the problem. You want to focus less on what your limbs are doing than on the damage that you're inflicting on your opponent. Punching and kicking also put you on the wrong side of the question — him or me? — by putting you in a defensive posture and keeping you at what feels like a safe, noncommittal distance. They pull your focus to the emotions going on inside of *you,* when where you really want to be is on the other side of the question, *inside of him.* That is where the solution to your problem lies — in him broken and screaming, you standing where he once was. When using your boots and bare hands to accomplish this—to break things inside of him and absolutely wreck him—you're going to need something more than your muscles. You'll need to recruit the largest amount of kE you can access: *your body weight in motion.* Without that powder charge of body weight in motion, you end up throwing bullets at him instead of shooting them. When your life is at stake, which would you rather do?

MASS, MOVEMENT, STRUCTURE, AND INTENT

The mechanics of striking—the intentional generation and balanced transfer of energy through your body weight in motion—drive every application for causing injury. Balanced body weight intentionally in motion is the powerhouse behind striking, the irresistible force behind joint breaking, and the explosive core of throwing. It's even the base engine of grabs and holds: a grab is simply a strike that ends with you holding on rather than letting go. When you strip out the base engine of striking, when you lose the power of body weight in motion, the potential for inflicting injury ceases to exist and you're back to rolling the dice and hoping for the best.

Mass

Mass is where the mechanics of striking begin. The simplest strike you can execute is falling on your enemy. That is a rudimentary transfer of energy through mass, by dropping your body weight, gaining energy through the power of gravity, and diffusing it entirely into the target—his body doing double duty as the energy-damping airbag that arrests your fall.

Every strike is based on this concept: a fall that is arrested and then transferred inside the target. To increase effectiveness and amplify the trauma, you simply add distance (the higher you fall from, the more energy you generate), specific targeting (groin, spine, skull, solar plexus) and appropriate tools (knees, boot heel). It's nearly artless, being barely more complicated than simply falling, but these minor additions begin to make all the difference as it relates to mass and injury—converting raw, unbridled energy into predictable, reproducible trauma. And as you learn to apply your mass effectively in this way, you start to make injury a one-way street, where your enemy feels like he just got hit by a bus, and all you feel is the gas pedal under your boot.

Movement

To understand movement in the context of violence, we also need to understand the concepts of potential and kinetic energy in relationship to injury.

Let's say you bend over and pick up a bowling ball. The bowling ball gains potential energy as you lift it (fig. 1). If it slips from your fingers and it begins to fall, the potential energy is converted into kinetic energy—the energy of motion. If the bowling ball lands on your foot, it will transfer the kinetic energy into your foot. The energy gets "spent" breaking your bones (fig. 2).

When you don't have a bowling ball, and you are striking with your body, the same principle holds. The bowling ball is your body. It stores potential energy (that is, energy that is potentially kinetic) in two forms: in chemical bonds inside

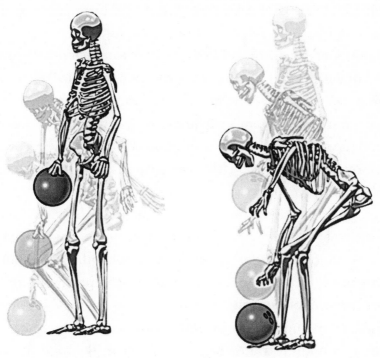

Figure 1   Figure 2

your muscles, and in the elevation of your mass in Earth's gravitational field. You can convert this potential energy to kinetic energy in two ways: using your muscles to accelerate your mass or lowering your mass in the gravitational field (like dropping the bowling ball).

In the most basic striking mechanics, this means stepping in and bending your knee(s) to strike. "Stepping in" is the acceleration of your mass through your muscles. (The phrase "step in" can be a little misleading, as it is more likely to manifest in real-world scenarios as lunging, driving, and body-slamming into your attacker, driving your entire mass into and through the target, his body, and the space he's standing in.)

"Bending the knee(s)" is about dropping your weight into the strike, letting gravity help you deliver force to the target.

This is a small and subtle movement when compared to the driving lunge. You don't want to bend your knee(s) past 90 degrees as it will be difficult for you to efficiently recover from a drop that low* and your opponent will likely react away from you faster and farther than you can follow. Instead, you want to bend your knee just enough to drop your weight into the strike while still maintaining a comfortable recovery so you can step in and strike him again, staying right on top of him the whole time.

I call this a drive-and-drop movement. If you've ever been to one of those Sky Zone–type trampoline parks—probably for a child's birthday party—you've seen this compound movement in action on a virtual loop. The person jumping on the trampoline will bend their knees at the bottom of their jump and then drive their mass outward in sync with the rebounding trampoline to send them sky high. It produces a rocket-like motion toward the ceiling. But at the bottom of a jump, have you ever seen someone bend their knees and then driven their body weight outward at an angle to move to the next trampoline? *They look like a guided missile,* like a bullet shot out of a gun, until they use their arms and legs to alter and slow their trajectory.

When you take this drive-and-drop movement out of the Sky Zone and into the battle zone and you apply it to a strike through a target on a human body, what you end up with is the most efficient and effective way to convert potential energy into kinetic energy, which can be used to inflict injury. The drive gives you a large vector of your weight in motion

---

* Next time you do standing lunges at the gym, try to come out of the bend with any kind of force—it's virtually impossible.

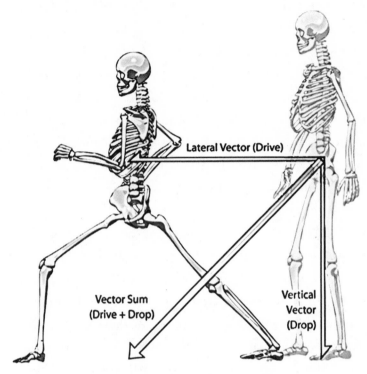

Figure 3

laterally. When you bend your knee as you strike you get another vector of your weight dropping straight down. Add those movements together, synchronously, and your opponent gets to eat a 45 degree–down vector strike. You become a guided missile (fig. 3).

It's not always one knee you will be bending, of course. Whether you bend one or both knees depends on what kind of strike you are doing: to put your fist through the solar plexus of a standing man, you will bend the leading knee into a forward stance; if he's lying on the ground, you'll bend both knees in a full stance to drop your weight into him.

Regardless of the type of strike, it is essential that your movement be unidirectional with complete follow-through.

When striking to injure, everything you have must move in a single direction into and through a single target. Pulling the arm or leg back out of the strike to "snap" it off (like many martial arts and combat sports teach) only means you're moving in a second, alternate (in this case opposite) direction, and that means you're not putting your all into wrecking your attacker. By definition, to achieve injury your body weight must move in the same direction as the strike—toward, in, and through the target.

If you are holding still or moving or leaning away from the strike, that lack of unidirectionality and follow-through precludes you from hitting as hard as you can. It's like trying to hit a home run by squaring to bunt. When you want to go deep, you make a full-throttle swing that nearly covers a 360 degree arc as you make contact and then follow all the way through. It is the follow-through of the swing, in fact, that completes the transfer of kinetic energy through the ball and out of the park.

The same principle applies to striking a violent predator coming at you. You are the bat and he is the ball. A big, juicy fastball right down the middle that you are going to drive-and-drop toward and through in a single direction with all your power.

Structure

Now you know to throw your entire body at your attacker, and drop your weight into him when you get there—stepping in, bending knees—to drive through him. The next piece of the physical puzzle is proper structure—in other words, being braced for impact.

This is a critical and often overlooked component of effective striking. Too often our tendency is to focus on how much force we can generate, and we forget to prepare for what happens when that force meets its target. It's an issue of basic physics. Newton's Third Law, to be precise: "Every action has an equal and opposite reaction." When you throw your body weight at your attacker and exert that force on him, an equal and opposite force will result, trying to push you backward, away from him. If your body is not structured properly to absorb that oppositional force, your strike won't stick and you'll bounce off your target.

Fortunately, good structure is straightforward and easy to evaluate. It starts from the ground up: foot, leg, hips, spine, shoulder, arm, fist (fig. 4).

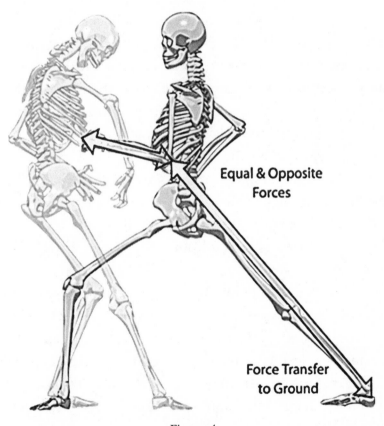

Figure 4

You want your feet planted flat on the ground, typically in a forward stance. Your back leg locked straight. Your hips square to your target. Your spine straight. Your upper arm squeezed to your side. Your forearm locked straight out. Your fist balled tight. With this structure, it is much harder to be moved off your position by the equal and opposite force your target will exert in response to your strike, because you're basically braced against the earth. To him, it's going to feel like he ran into a concrete-filled steel post. He'll be the only one moving away. And from there you'll be free to step in again as a single, solid unit—like a battering ram—and continue raining ruination down upon him.

Just remember: structure will always buckle at the weak point. You can have everything aligned perfectly taut and tight, but if the heel of your planted foot is off the ground, that's where your structure will blow out. You'll strike him and get driven back on that wobbly foot, perhaps losing your balance. And the more you move away from the strike, the less effective it will be.

Intent

The final piece of the base engine is the motor itself, the thing that drives us to send our body weight through our human target: *intent*.

As I've said throughout this book, intent is typically the only differentiating factor between the average person and the criminal sociopath. The sociopath has no qualms about hurting people, and wants it to the exclusion of all else. The normal, socialized human doesn't *want* to hurt anybody. But we're not talking about "want" here. The point of this book is to prepare you for the unlikely, black swan event of asocial violence where what you *want* is irrelevant and what you *need* is of paramount importance.

You have all the knowledge, all the tools. Now you *need* the intent to employ them because it is intent, ultimately, that makes the difference. Intent—the focus of all your efforts—drives striking. Without it, striking becomes half-hearted and limp. It lacks spine and prevents positive results. It is flaccid motion devoid of commitment.

When you strip all the social baggage away, intent is nothing more than the business-like execution of a single-minded goal: the infliction of injury to save your life. A strike driven home with the intent to knock your assailant into the ICU gets the job done. A strike with the *hope* of discouraging him from hurting you does not. The will to injure him is the spark that fuses all your assets and your efforts—your body weight in motion, your structure—into a single terrible unit that will hit him with everything you have.

IN RHYTHM AND ON TIME

I don't want you just to be comfortable and effective with the tool of violence. I want you to be explosively efficient. Have you ever read a spy novel and heard the writer talk about a bone breaking with "a satisfying crunch?" That seems like a strange, dark feeling, but I want you to get to a place where you can relate to that. Where your training creates an expectation that, if ever challenged, you'll know what's supposed to happen as a result of your actions. I want any violent predator foolish enough to target you to regret ever crossing your path—but only after they've regained consciousness. *If* they regain consciousness. The way that happens is by striking your enemy multiple times, with perfect rhythm and perfect timing.

Striking with rhythm is just like it sounds: striking an opponent repeatedly with a steady beat as if you're following the tick of a metronome only you can hear, tolling out his doom—one—injury—at—a—time. It begins with the weight drop we discussed earlier in this chapter. You drop your weight to fire off a strike backed with momentum, then you raise it again to reload your potential energy reservoir for the next strike. This rise and fall over time generates a waveform. This waveform is the basis of rhythmic striking.

Getting into a rhythm this way does two things: It allows you to take full advantage of your opponent being in Effect state as a result of the initial injury, and it maximizes your efficiency in following up on your first strike.

Injury, if you recall, creates a spinal reflex reaction in its sufferer that leaves him incapable of voluntary movement for some period. Rhythmic striking allows you to injure your opponent again before the reaction runs its course and he regains the use of the uninjured parts of his body. Once you start in on him like that, you are the one who gets to decide you're done with him. One injury follows the next, neatly in lockstep. There's no hesitation, no looking for the next opening, no waiting to see what happens next, no flailing around ineffectually. No wasted time whatsoever. This cycle of compounding injury, therefore, sets up an inescapable death-spiral. From the first injury to the last, your opponent has no say in the matter. No counters, no retaliation, no escape. Just a steady, rhythmic, breaking of his body, decrementing its functions until he's no longer a threat.

You can enhance your rhythmic striking by actually using a metronome, set to a moderate pace of forty beats per minute, while training with a partner. Your goal is to cause an injury on every beat. Every time it clicks you want to be driving a strike through a target, breaking a joint, and/or throwing your partner. You will move between beats, slowly, so that the injury occurs on the beat. At first this might not seem very slow—forty beats per minute means one strike every 1.5 seconds—but that's a lifetime compared to real-world violence. Jorge Orozco took Officer Michelle Jeter to the ground and landed nine vicious blows to her head in *less than nine seconds*. The Nuestra Familia assassin stabbed the shotcaller multiple times in five seconds. Still, if you find yourself falling behind, or having to use bursts of speed to keep up, slow the metronome down until you can move smoothly from one injury to the next. When in doubt, slower is always better. Remember: slow is smooth, smooth is fast, fast is deadly.

You should always train at the rate where you are in complete control of your base striking mechanics, because aside from contributing to getting into rhythm, control is essential to good timing. A groin injury, for example, will cause a man to bring his head down with his chin out, exposing it to an uncontested uppercut. Imagine, though, how much more damage you could do if you met his chin with the uppercut *just* as he was snapping his head down into it! This is the basic idea of timing—making things happen when it is most advantageous to have them happen—and it is a natural complement to the concept of rhythm striking. In fact, the cultivation of good timing is the point of developing rhythm, because together they open targets, maximize your efficiency, and compound your enemy's injuries.

None of this should distract from the most basic truth in striking: body weight in motion is *the* terrible engine that causes injury. Pull out the base engine of striking, remove body weight from the equation, and you're going nowhere. Take body weight out and countering and blocking by your opponent become possible, the likelihood of injury evaporates, and the chances of saving your own life go with it.

Body weight in motion crushes and ruptures tissue. Body weight in motion tears out joints. Body weight in motion propels people to the ground. You can spend years learning thousands of techniques, but if you don't have body weight behind them, you're not going to hurt anyone. When your life's on the line, that's not okay. So get everything you have, everything you are, in there. Don't settle for the weight of your arm, or leg. Use your entire mass to wreck him, whether it's a traditional single strike, a joint-break, or a throw.

JOINT-BREAKING 101

The lever is the simplest machine, and one that has been utilized by humans forever—especially when you consider that our bodies are full of them. The human skeleton is a fine example of the power of levers—an ode to mechanical advantage writ in bone and sinew. Levers are the basis of human movement—and are therefore used constantly in violence. They magnify the power of strikes, they allow a small person to throw a much larger one, and they give us the ability to generate and transmit the forces necessary to break joints.

Understanding what makes a lever—its parts and how dif-

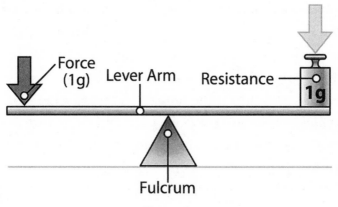

Figure 5

ferent arrangements of the parts have different advantages—will allow you to tell whether you can break a given joint from where you are, with what you've got.

There are three parts to a lever: *fulcrum, force,* and *resistance* (fig. 5). The fulcrum is the point that the lever arm pivots or turns on; the force is where effort is applied at a distance from the fulcrum; while the resistance acts on the other side of the fulcrum.

The only thing you need to remember about levers is this: *force applied to one end of the lever is transferred across the lever arm, resulting in work done on the resistance at the other end of the lever.* Simply put, pushing on one end makes things happen at the other. In the context of violence and injury, that means breaking or tearing out a joint.

What does it mean when I say we are tearing out a joint? I know, that phrase sounds very savage and un-technical. What I mean is that you are tearing the strong bands of connective tissue that hold the joint together and allow it to function. You are tearing ligaments and snapping tendons.

Ligaments are tough, fibrous bands of tissue that connect bone to bone. When you tear ligaments, the alignment of the bones on either end of the joint is compromised, making the joint more likely to dislocate, and less likely to work properly.

Tendons are the ropes that lash muscles to bones, allowing the joint to move. The tendon-to-bone connection is so strong that sometimes the bone itself will fail before the tendon or muscle tears, resulting in a sliver of bone peeling off. Either way, when you tear tendons, the muscles can no longer pull on the bones and the joint cannot move properly.

To break a joint, you must use leverage to drive it past its pathological limits—that is, the point at which the joint "locks out." The lockout position is the end of that joint's natural range of motion. Any movement beyond that point is where the damage begins. Pushing beyond that pathological limit is the only way to ensure that you tear tendons and/or ligaments. It is the only way to break a joint.

Breaking a joint is not easy. It doesn't just happen because you'd like it to. Tendons and ligaments are very tough; joints themselves are put together to minimize the chances of getting torn out or broken. To overcome these factors, it's going to take everything you have—your mind and body working in conjunction with physical law—to get it done.

All the intent in the world, driving all those body weight forces you've harnessed, will come to naught, in fact, without a good, solid lever arm to send those forces against. There has to be meaningful resistance on the other end to create the proper leverage, and the fulcrum to pivot yourself against. Without that mechanical advantage, all the force of will you can generate gets dissipated into so much heat and noise. And while that can be dramatic, it doesn't get you that broken joint.

When petite Bonnie incapacitated her larger attacker, she used the resistance of his body weight to identify the fulcrum point (the knee) along the lever arm (his plant leg) through which she would send the full force of her body weight by way of a heel strike. The result was a complete, catastrophic knee injury that put her attacker down for good.

Shawn used the bottom of the car door as his fulcrum and gravity on his downed assailant as his resistance. The injury came when he grabbed hold of the man's foot and applied upward force, letting the car door do all the dirty work.

GETTING A JOINT-BREAK DONE

Now that you know what it takes to break a joint—intent, force and a lever arm—let's look at some of the details that make sure you can get it done.

Prior Trauma

No one is going to let you walk up and grab their hand, set up leverage, and break their wrist. You're going to have to injure him first. Both Bonnie and Shawn inflicted an initial injury before delivering the strike that incapacitated their attackers. Gouge him in the eye, kick him in the groin, strike him in the liver or the kidneys, it doesn't matter. Just make sure you injure him sufficiently *before* you go in for the joint-break that puts him out of commission. Remember, it is only injury that will induce the spinal reflex reaction that will render him unable to prevent you from breaking the joint of your choice.

Quality of the Lever Arm

A flexible lever arm is no good for getting work done. You need a rigid structure to transfer force across if you're going to snap that joint. Two things will help ensure this happens: isolating the bones of the lever arm, and a tight grip on the end of it. This is precisely what Shawn did when he got his attacker's straightened leg and secured his grip on the foot before wrenching it skyward toward the bottom of the car door.

Imagine kicking your attacker in the groin to create the prior trauma you need to grab his hand and break his wrist. He does a textbook groin reaction—knees buckled, bent over, chin up—and then proceeds to collapse onto the ground on his side. If you had a casual grip on his wrist you're probably going to lose his hand. If you crush his hand in your fist and he goes down, you're going to keep control of it and apply enough force against the resistance offered by his slumped-over body to get what you want—a broken wrist.

Crushing his hand in your fist also causes the hand to behave like a solid unit rather than many smaller flexible units. This allows you to isolate the bones in the lever arm (in this case, his actual arm) and minimize movement in nearby joints as you engage the joint you want to break (the wrist). Imagine trying to break his wrist by grabbing several of his fingers. As you apply force, the joints of his fingers would eat up that force as each individual joint bent. In the end, the force finally reaching the wrist would be far too small to break it.

To get a broken wrist you need to make sure that the wrist

is the only joint that's going to be allowed to move. Just the wrist—not the whole hand. Having a solid lever arm isn't the only factor in the transfer of forces, however.

Setting the Leverage

Set the leverage close to your center of gravity to ensure that you're using more body weight than muscular strength. With your hands out away from your body, you lose leverage and less body weight can be transferred. When you drop your weight with your arms out, some force is used up in bending your shoulders and the transfer of force is sloppy. With your hands in close to your center of gravity (pelvis), you can use muscular strength to hang on tight while you drop your weight to break the joint.

Keep Your Back Straight

Keeping your back straight when dropping your weight brings more of your weight into the lever. If you bend your spine, rounding your back, you are only dropping the weight of your arms and upper torso into the leverage. This is only half of you. Drop the whole hammer on him—keep your back straight and bend your knees to drop your weight.

Apply Force in the Optimal Direction

This may seem like a no-brainer, but it's a detail people often miss. Imagine you want to lever a big rock out of the ground. The most efficient way to do this is to push straight down on your end, to lever the rock straight up against gravity at the other. If you apply your force at an angle other than straight down, however, say at 45 degrees to the vertical (pushing sideways as you push down), some of your force is going to be wasted trying to move the lever sideways. In fact, the force could cause the lever to slip out from under the rock, wasting your time and effort.

This works the same way in joint breaking. If you want to break an elbow by locking it straight and hyperextending it, you need to apply the force straight down into the elbow along the same plane that the elbow would bend up through its normal arc. If you apply force at an angle to this plane, the efficiency of your leverage is reduced. In fact, if the angle is far enough off, the elbow will simply bend in its normal arc instead of breaking.

And then you're in real trouble, because now a violent predator realizes you might not know what you're doing.

THE SIX BASE LEVERAGES

All joints break the same way—by moving past the patho-logical limit and tearing the tissues that hold the joint together. But where is that pathological limit? And what's the best way to move a joint to get there, and go beyond?

That's where the six base leverages come in: six different directions to break every joint in the human body. Every joint-lock or joint-manipulation technique that you have heard of, seen, or experienced is one of these six base leverages or a combination of two or more. In fact, every possible way to break a joint can be derived from the six base leverages, which is why I focus on these instead of techniques. The leverages are the rules of multiplication; the techniques are the multiplication table.

These leverages are based on the three degrees of freedom every mobile joint has—bending, twisting, rocking to the side—and the ability to move forward or backward in that manner. These are the principles of joint-breaking, and each one has its own distinct, physiological name:*

1. Extension (bending forward, or "straightening")
2. Flexion (bending backward, or "bending")
3. Supination (twisting or rotating away from the body)
4. Pronation (twisting or rotating toward the body)
5. Adduction (rocking away from the body)
6. Abduction (rocking toward the body)

Here is a simple exercise to help you remember all six base leverages by moving through them in sequence. Start with your left hand out in front of you, palm down, fingers pointing away from you. Now:

Bend your wrist so your fingers point at the ceiling, palm away from you, like you're motioning for someone to stop. *This is extension.*

Bend your wrist in the opposite direction, so your hand folds down, fingers pointing toward the floor, palm toward you, like you're showing someone your new engagement ring. *This is flexion.*

With your hand in flexion, rotate your forearm so your fingers point at the ceiling, palm still toward you. Keep rotating

---

* The physiological and anatomical terminology of joint movement is a confusing mish-mash. For the sake of simplicity (and sanity) for our students and our readers, we've created our own taxonomy that focuses merely on the essence of each movement.

to try and point your thumb at the floor. Your elbow will want to bend slightly. *This is supination.*

From supination, rotate your forearm 270 degrees in the opposite direction so your fingers point away from you off to your left, palm toward you. Your elbow will straighten. If you were to put your arm behind you when you did this, it would be the same motion you make to put your arm through a jacket sleeve. *This is pronation.*

Move your hand back to the starting position (palm down, fingers pointing ahead of you). Keeping your palm parallel to the floor, rock your hand out to your left, trying to point your fingers to your left, like you're sliding cards across a table or like a DJ scratches a record. *This is adduction.*

Now rock your hand back the other way, keeping your palm down and parallel to the floor, trying to point your fingers to your right. *This is abduction.*

Did you feel the tightness in the wrist joint at the end of each of these motions? That's the edge of the pathological limit for your wrist in each of those six directions. If you continue the motion beyond that tightness, with enough force, you will tear the joint out.

KNOW YOUR PATHOLOGICAL LIMITS

Now you know every possible direction in which a joint can be broken. That knowledge is only partially useful, however. What makes it fully applicable is knowing *how far* you have to force each joint in each respective direction in order to break or tear it out. That is what this section covers.

Extension (Straightening)

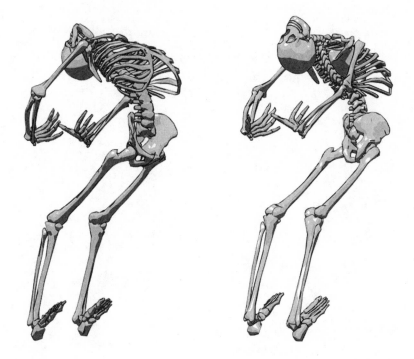

This is the state of most joints in the human body when standing erect—most joints are naturally ready to break through hyperextension.

Ankle:	20° (called "dorsiflexion")
Knee:	15°
Hip:	30°
Fingers/Toes:	50°
Wrist:	70° (dorsiflexion)
Elbow:	15°
Shoulder:	45°
Spine:	30°
Neck:	55°

So, to break the knee with extension, for example, you need to make it bend backwards farther than 15 degrees. A stomp to the front of the knee will make it move 90 degrees in the wrong direction—making him sit down like a flamingo. This is more than enough to tear it out.

Flexion (Bending)

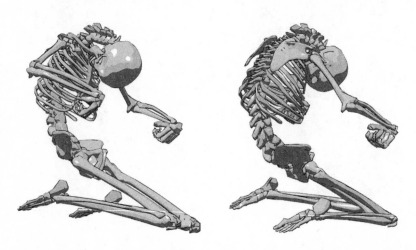

This is bending the joint and then compressing it beyond its range of motion. Note that fewer joints are susceptible to breaking in this direction—typically because the body "runs into itself" and ceases further motion in the joint.

Ankle:	45° (called "plantar flexion")
Knee:	130°
Fingers/Toes:	30–110°
Wrist:	80–90°
Spine:	75°
Neck:	70–90°

To break a knee with flexion, you need to bend it beyond

a 130-degree arc—not easy to do. This becomes easier when you add a big fat fulcrum into the crook of his knee for the knee joint to bend around—like your fist, a baton, or his other shin. Now the knee will separate and tear out more readily.

Supination (Rotating from Inside to Outside)

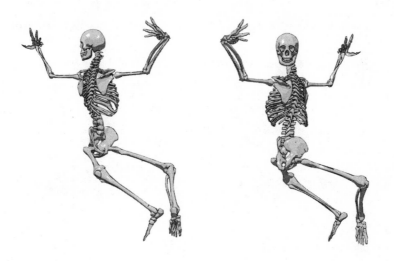

This is getting rotation inside of the joint by cranking on a lever (typically at 90 degrees to the axis of rotation) outward, away from the centerline of the body.

Ankle:	0° (ankle isolation difficult)
Knee:	40°
Hip:	45°
Fingers/Toes:	25°
Wrist:	90° (rotates at elbow, injury at wrist)
Shoulder:	70° horizontally (vertical flexion: 180°)
Spine:	70°

To tear out the knee using supination—with the victim on his back, for example—you could grab his foot and snap-rotate it outward. Any rotation past 40 degrees will tear the knee. Note that the ankle is notoriously difficult to isolate in supination. Forces put into the ankle will translate upward into the knee first, before it ruptures the ankle because the knee is the weakest structure in the leg system, and the weakest point always fails first. In the case of supination it will always be inside the knee that goes, then the ankle or hip—all of which are debilitating.

Pronation (Rotating from Outside to Inside)

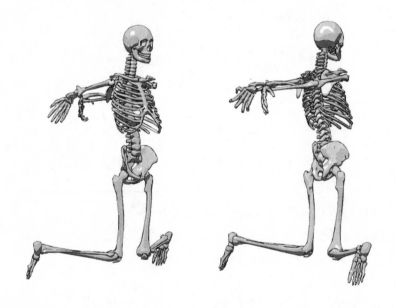

This is getting rotation inside of the joint by cranking on a lever (typically at 90 degrees to the axis of rotation) inward toward the centerline of the body.

Ankle: 0° (ankle isolation is difficult)
Knee: 10°

Hip:	40°
Finger/Toes:	25°
Wrist:	90° (rotates at elbow, injury at wrist)
Shoulder:	110° horizontally (vertical extension: 60°)

To tear out the knee using pronation—again with the victim lying on his back as an example—you could grab his foot and snap-rotate it inward. Pronation of the leg is significantly more limited than supination. Any rotation past 10 degrees will tear the knee, which means injury is quicker than with supination if you apply enough force. Just as with supination, though, the ankle is notoriously difficult to isolate in pronation so any forces applied there will translate upward into the knee before affecting the ankle.

Adduction (Rocking to the Outside)

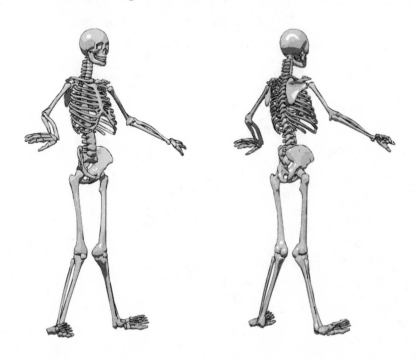

This is rocking or bending sideways toward the pinky side of your hand (in the wrist).

Ankle:	30° (called "pronation/inversion")
Knee:	0°
Fingers/Toes:	30°
Wrist:	30–50° (called "ulnar deviation")

A simple way to break a knee using adduction would be to stomp on the knee from the outside, breaking it sideways into his center. This is the classic chill-your-blood football injury—though because the knee has no range of motion in this direction, the force doesn't need to be massive to be effective. When Bernard Pollard hit Tom Brady on the side of the knee in Week 1 of the 2008 NFL season and knocked him out for the year, Pollard was on the ground and dove from his knees to make contact. There was no massive, full-speed collision. That's how brittle the knee is during adduction: it doesn't bend, it just breaks.

Abduction (Rocking to the inside)

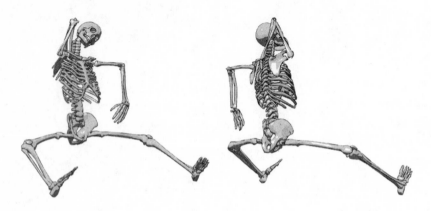

This is rocking or bending sideways toward the thumb side of your hand (in the wrist).

Ankle:	20° (called "supination/eversion")
Knee:	0°
Hip:	45–50°
Fingers/Toes:	30°
Wrist:	20° (called "radial deviation".)
Shoulder:	180°
Spine:	35°

To break a knee using abduction would be to stomp on the knee from the inside, breaking it sideways to the outside. Once again, the knee has no range of motion in this direction, but unlike adduction it is not an injury you typically see on the football field unless a player's cleats catch in the turf. Otherwise a hit from the inside simply sends the player's legs skyward.

Now you know that there is one fundamental way to break a joint—move the joint past its pathological limit—and there are only six ways to get it there—the three degrees of freedom (bending, twisting, rocking) both forward and back. Just six base leverages to break every joint in the human body. And you know them all.

It doesn't matter what body part you use to apply the force, or if it's even a body part at all: you can use your hands, feet, hip, or shoulder, or a briefcase, car door, the curb. If the leverage is set properly, the joint will break.

That said, break it as soon as you grab it. Don't monkey around. The longer it takes you to get a hold of the lever arm, isolate the bones, and set the leverage to get it done, the longer your enemy has to get past his initial spinal reflex and kill you. Break it now. If for some reason you can't get it done, let it go and immediately strike another target. Injure him again to keep him busy and then try again to break it. Just because you want to break a joint doesn't mean that's all you can do. As long as you are alive and mobile, *you always have options.*

THROWING 101

Gravity and hard surfaces probably cause more accidental injury than every other method combined. Simply falling — solo, with no help from another person — can result in some trivial embarrassment, or it can, in the rare occasion when everything lines up just right, cause death.

If we add another person into the equation — someone to shove, trip, or otherwise knock down the victim — willful use of gravity and hard surfaces can function as a tool for violence. Now we are throwing people. Of course, a throw — no matter how simple or complicated, how cool or mundane — is only as good as the injuries it inflicts.

It's tempting to look at throwing as a specialized art, its own discipline, removed from other aspects of violence. A throw looks like nothing else. It's much easier to see the connection between striking and joint breaking. Stomping an ankle looks like a strike, as does hammering the back of an elbow to break it. But a throw…a throw *must be* a special technique, unlike any other method of injury.

Throwing is nothing more than a special case of striking. Striking, as we define it, is applying body weight in motion through an anatomical target to break it. When that target is a joint at the pathological limit, we get a joint break. For throwing, the only change is in the target. Instead of a piece of anatomy, it becomes your adversary's balance, with the goal of disrupting that balance to initiate and accelerate a fall—an aimed and assisted collision with the ground, typically isolating a specific piece of anatomy or cluster of targets (like the head) for that collision. Instead of smashing ourselves through that anatomy (as in a basic strike) we're going to smash the anatomy against the ground.

Once again, I'm not interested in complicated techniques that you have to memorize. The answer to the question, "What's the best throw?" is, and will always be: "The one that puts the man down so he can't get back up." Instead of the crowd-pleasing, super-impressive throws that only the most coordinated, athletic, and highly trained could ever hope to achieve, I am going to share with you the base principles that drive purposeful, useful throwing.

Practically speaking, throwing is as simple as knocking people down. It's doing the work of a patch of ice or a crack in the sidewalk. It's simply recognizing a situation that would cause someone to struggle to maintain balance. The moment at the top of that last step on a set of stairs, when their body weight is out of balance—the moment when, if you needed to, you could give them a good, hearty shove down the staircase without much effort.

At a very basic level, throws involve recognizing opportunities to manipulate balance into a fall, and seeing a through-path from where you both are now into either a slip or a trip. If he's already moving, he's already falling—catching himself is a matter of him getting his legs back under him. Sticking your shoe in his gears, either by preventing him from getting his feet under him or knocking him down, is technically a throw. With two bodies in motion you don't really have time to sort through a mass of techniques looking for just the right one—you need to be able to take full advantage of where you're both going to break his structure and put him down.

While throwing doesn't take as much effort as you might think, it does take a little bit of know-how, as well as some setup. Fortunately, throwing people into the ground also gives us some big payback for the relative (small) effort—namely, head trauma. It's the only way, absent a weapon, that we can get directly at the brain. We're going for concussion, skull fracture, and serious head injuries—bleeding in the brain. On the way there we'll almost certainly get some other injuries. Going headfirst into the ground with all his body weight over him isn't going to do your opponent's neck any good, so cervical injuries are a real possibility. Not to mention the injuries he'll sustain when he reaches out to break his fall—sprains, dislocations, and breaks of the hand, wrist, elbow, and shoulder are possibilities. He can also end up with the same kinds of injuries to his legs, even broken bones if he lands awkwardly.

Furthermore, injured people operate particularly poorly on the ground. The standing person can very easily engage more body weight against the downed man, through stomps and knee drops, upping the severity of further trauma.

In this regard, throwing could be seen almost as an injury multiplier that magnifies your efforts. A single strike applied through your attacker's structure can get you multiple life-threatening injuries, put him into a vulnerable position, and allow you to really ramp up whatever you do next in order to survive your life-or-death encounter. That's a lot of gain for a single strike. The punch to the throat, by comparison, gets you a single injury that will take time to manifest fully. If you can recognize the opportunity and seize it, a throw can shorten your encounter to the blink of an eye.

Technically speaking, all throws, from the simplest takedown to the most complex example of "free flying lessons" arise from the same set of rules—simple, easy rules anyone can remember, recognize, and master.

THE COMPONENTS OF A THROW

If you only utilize the most basic requirements for a throw— intent, prior injury, and body weight—what you really end up doing is shoving an injured man to the ground. While not a bad way to start tipping the odds in your favor, it's not optimal, either. There's nothing—other than perhaps an injury you've already inflicted—that says he couldn't conceivably catch his balance and arrest his fall, or fail to break anything important when he hits the ground.

That's not good enough when your life is on the line. A real combat throw is more than a happy accident—it's making the fall as destructive as possible to your assailant. To do that you need to break his structure, take his balance, aim your target at the ground, and accelerate his fall.

Break His Structure

All things being equal, your enemy would prefer to stand with his center of gravity stacked on top of his legs. When everything sits nice and neat like this—center of gravity over legs over base—he can easily maintain his balance and move his weight around at will. You want to break his structure by knocking one of these pieces out of alignment. That can mean buckling his leg so he starts to collapse, or knocking his center of gravity past his feet so things aren't stacked up so nice and neat anymore. Imagine kicking a leg out from under a stool, knocking the stool over. This is your body weight striking through either his base or his center of gravity to get him moving or make him vulnerable to a fall.

Take His Balance

Starting the fall usually happens in conjunction with breaking your opponent's structure, but not always. Take his balance and use it to wreck him—but don't inadvertently give it back. In other words, don't break his structure and then grab on to him and hold him up so that he has a chance to regain his balance. Keep him moving into the throw, with the new equilibrium of balance occurring when he smacks down at the end.

Aim the Target at the Ground

Isolate a single body part for impact. The head is the ideal target, but it can also be a single shoulder (from the side), the scapula (shoulder blade), the coccyx (tailbone), even the spine. Aim, in this case, is a two-part deal, with an "X marks the spot" on the ground and a projectile (the anatomical target) that you're hurling at that X. (Of course, the specific X that you choose doesn't matter—what matters is visualizing directing your opponent into the ground, and choosing an imaginary X can help.) Your job is to make sure the two connect as precisely, and as violently, as you can.

Accelerate His Fall

Accelerating his fall is all about adding your body weight to the mix. This is one of the features that makes throwing so devastating: ideally, you'll have his body weight in motion for the strike, and yours on top of it, finishing it off. This doubles his mass for the fall and final impact. Imagine weighing 400 pounds and striking an opponent with fists of concrete. That's the level of force you can achieve with a well-executed throw. Also, accelerating him into the throw screws with the timing of his catch-fall reflex. Chances are his arm will be late for the party, though his brain will get there just in time.

Using these specific protocols, we can turn any shove-and-fall accident into an effective combat throw with minimal training. If you grab the injured man by the hair, or neck, and buckle his leg by driving through it with your own and then ride his head down into the concrete with your entire mass—either shoving it away to accelerate and bounce it off the ground or simply landing on it—you have performed a targeted and controlled sequence of events that make serious head injury as likely as possible. Instead of shoving and hoping for the best, now you're taking charge of the situation, leaving nothing to chance, replacing all the variables with constants, and increasing your chances of survival and escape.

THE TWO TYPES OF THROWS: SLIPS AND TRIPS

There are two principal ways to go when we break our opponent's structure and take his balance. We can either blast his base out from under his center of gravity, or push his center of gravity so it falls outside his base. This produces two basic types of throws: slips and trips.

Slips are just like Charlie Brown trying to kick the football and falling as it's yanked away—his feet shoot out from under his center of gravity and he falls. Slips are the least robust of the two type of throws, simply because there are only so many ways to knock someone's feet out from under them: pushing, pulling, or kicking one or both of his legs. The simplest operational expression of this idea is the leg sweep.

Depending on where your opponent's weight is, and which leg you have access to, you have to make a determination whether to pick up his leg to get him off balance or kick it out. A leg that is not bearing weight, whether due to injury or the fact that you're catching it mid-stride is easy to hook, pick up, push, or pull to take him down. In that case, you're simply moving the weight of his leg outside of where he expected to land it and the rest of him falls as a result.

However, if he does have his weight on the leg you can reach, you're not going to be able to do any of that. The leg will stick, anchored to the ground by his mass. In that case, you're going to have to strike it out from under him with your entire mass, using something akin to a shin kick or full body check while violently displacing his feet out from under him with yours.

Most of the time with a mobile attacker it's obvious which leg is bearing weight, but many times it's not. It's important to at least figure it out, so you can choose the proper method for taking that leg out from under him. The basic rule of thumb is:

If you're attacking the stepping leg—> sweep
If you're attacking the standing leg—> strike

When in doubt though, just blast through it with a strike. Technique and nuance be damned. If the leg has little or no weight on it (meaning it was "sweepable") you'll knock it out from under him and drop him, no sweat. If he was standing on it after all, it won't matter because you've directed all of your body weight in one direction, with full force, right through a target.

A drawback of slips, especially leg sweeps, if that's all you're doing—taking his feet out from under him—is that then you aren't targeting a specific piece of anatomy for the collision with the ground. You'll produce an uncontrolled fall, for both of you, that leaves resulting injury up to chance. Absent prior injury, it's equally likely that he smacks his head or that he has enough wherewithal to be able to protect his brain.

If he gets his hands out in time his reflexes will save his head, and then you have to hope for sprained or broken wrists, jammed shoulders, and the like. Maybe he'll get the wind knocked out of him, but maybe he won't. All told, slips like a leg sweep are not terribly reliable unless you've gone the extra mile, like grabbing him by the neck to ensure that as you kick his leg out from under him you'll be hurling his head at the ground as he goes down. Without such measures, leg sweeps are a spin of the injury roulette wheel— sometimes a good number comes up, sometimes it doesn't. So, either make it happen or be prepared to stay right on top of him, putting more injury into him when he hits the ground.

Trips, by contrast, are like that infamous crack in the sidewalk—the feet catch briefly, holding still long enough for the center of gravity to fall outside the base and send the person headfirst into the ground. Pretty much every pratfall you've ever seen a physical comedian do that didn't involve slipping on a banana peel is some version of a trip. Trips are a much larger family of throws than slips because there are multitudes of ways to make a person's center of gravity fall outside their base, knocking them down.

From the very simple "hip push" (to drive his pelvis past his feet and into the ground) to the more advanced shoulder throw (replacing his base with yours and then making him fall outside it on your terms), to base-break throws, drop throws, and hip throws, there is an arsenal of trips at your disposal to help achieve incapacitating injury.

Base-break throws are those where you break the opponent's balance by attacking and breaking the structure holding him up. This can be as a stomp through the ankle or knee, breaking the joint, or it can mean applying your body weight to buckle his leg (rather than simply smash straight through it) and drag his center of gravity out past his base. Obviously, this is also a strike and a joint-break, but it fulfills our definition of a throw as well.

Drop throws are where you attach your mass to your opponent and lie down to throw him off balance. Imagine putting your shin through a man's groin, then grabbing him by the neck and lying down in front of him to body-slam his head into the concrete. He'll hit as if he weighed twice as much, and it'll be twice as ugly as doing it all by himself.

Drop throws come in two basic varieties: attaching yourself to the top of the opponent's spine by grabbing the hair, head, neck, lapels, shoulders, or arms, and attaching yourself to the bottom end of his spine by grabbing the hips or knees (usually from behind him). In either case, you are dragging his center of gravity out beyond his base and using it to accelerate his fall into the ground.

Hip throws got their name from the use of the hip as a fulcrum point for the throw. The victim is kicked up into the air by the hip and rounds the hip on his way into the fall. While the hip is indeed the fulcrum point for the throw, the legs are the primary actors in providing power for the maneuver. The hip is more properly the contact point upon which you'll balance his center of gravity. A better way of understanding the hip throw, and how it is indeed a trip, is to look at it this way: you're replacing his base with yours, taking him off his feet while balancing him over your own, and then making him fall outside your base.

Shoulder throws are similar to hip throws with the fulcrum point at the shoulder instead of the hip. What we get out of this is a hip throw with an added lever arm the length of your spine. This takes your opponent through a longer arc, resulting in a higher throw, which gives you more time to accelerate him through the fall from a greater height. When we couple this with an Earth-shattering "John Henry" swing of your arms slapping him down by his arm, we get the most powerful throw possible. Especially if you drop to one knee, pulling him down out of the sky as you go, to ride him down with your mass.

This throw gets you so much hang time and projection you can throw a man upside down through a plate-glass window, or into/onto/through anything else in your environment—the curb, a fire hydrant, traffic. In training, I've seen lights cleared off the ceiling by the victim's feet. Much like the hip throw, if you know what you're doing, it's well worth the effort.

I know that's a lot of different throws, but my intention is not to make your head swim, it's only to show you what is possible, what is sitting latent inside you now that you have the knowledge and the know-how as it relates to all forms of striking.

The key is in recognizing what all these things have in common and then keeping things simple. Just as every joint only breaks one way, so it is with throwing. There's only one throw—someone falling. That fall can be caused in only one of two ways, making his feet come out from under him or making him fall outside his feet. Everything else is just detail work. In other words, don't overthink it. It's still just striking, only this time we're using the entire planet.

WE'RE USING THE PLANET, BUT THIS ISN'T PLANET FITNESS

In the last chapter I talked about the virtues of training slow. It is critical for perfecting all aspects of the tool of violence, particularly striking for the purposes of injury. But if you think going slow means easy, soft, light, and painless, you're dead wrong. Slow means correct—spot-on targeting, constantly driving your body weight through the opponent's structure to buckle it, full follow-through. When it's done right, it's methodically cruel and, yes, can even result in you suffering some painful bruises. As it should be.

There's a huge difference between pain and injury. Pain hurts, and then it's gone. Injury is lingering and long-lasting. Pain in training tells you that what's happening would be truly terrible at full speed; it reminds you what you're here for. If you know what to do with it, pain can help you focus your efforts and fan the flames of your intent to injure in time to save your life.

If I hit the mats for a painless hour and walk off not feeling like I've been in a fight, without a mark on me the next day, I might as well have gone to Planet Fitness and knocked out some reps on the squat rack instead. I hit the mats to feel it, not play at it or pretend. For the next couple of days I carry with me the badges of honor that show I trained hard for violence: bruises, scratches, the marks that training knives leave on the body.

The ones that make me proudest are the most accurate and controlled, like dime-sized contusions precisely over my heart, because that means the training is dialing in. Training, after all, is about precision, and precision is about learning control. Control means that everything is tight, focused, and right at the edge without tumbling over. I want my training partner to have total control over what I'm doing and where I'm going at all times during his turn, so I don't get dumped on my head, thrown haphazardly onto one shoulder, or get something broken because he held it loosely and went for the target with sloppy technique.

When he gets it right it's going to hurt; even going slow, he's going to put one bony square inch of him through one square inch of me, meaning my rib cage will bounce off his elbow, and not the other way around. If his structure is properly immovable, it should feel like I ran into a steel knob at the top of a concrete-filled post.

I'm going to do the same to him on my turn, because anything less is screwing around, and sloppiness could get you killed out there. I must practice with total precision and control, so I can drive that head anywhere—straight into the concrete in the real world, or tucked under for a roll, in training. I'll tuck it on the mats, exactly, and I'll pile-drive it outside, precisely—getting exactly what I want instead of hoping for the best.

They say that pain is a great teacher, and I know this for a fact; I seek nothing but instruction every time I hit the mats. I've learned that what we do works, I've learned that pain can't stop me, and I've learned to use it to focus my intent.

SURVIVING SURVIVAL

We've discussed—in sometimes queasy detail—just what it's likely to look like and feel like if you, say, tear out an opponent's knee joint. We've considered just how much force and intent it takes to achieve that level of damage. We've done that because entering a fight for your life without that intent will get you nowhere—but also because thinking clinically about the human body and its vulnerabilities is good for your peace of mind *after* the fact of violent conflict, as well.

Think of it this way: What happens *after* survival? When you've put yourself successfully through a violent predator and are now standing where they once stood? You're mobile and they are incapacitated. You are alive and they are dead.

The most sensitive and skeptical of my new students and seminar attendees often ask me some version of that question. They've read or heard dozens of stories in the news and online about PTSD and survivor's guilt, nightmares, and regret. Soldiers—true heroes—who come home afraid to go to sleep, haunted by the question of "why him and not me?" Police officers who have pulled the trigger on mentally ill attackers who were imminent threats to their families or their neighbors.

These scared students don't want to be haunted. They don't want to die at the hands of an asocial predator, to be sure, but their desire to be free of guilt and shame and torment can feel equally strong. They think that understanding the tool of violence and training to effectively deploy it will increase the likelihood of all those things happening. Not so much that they will be turned into aggressive predators themselves, more that by choosing to study violence they are inviting violence into their lives at a karmic level.

I understand this point of view. I get where it comes from. The reality is, though, that it is understanding the principles of violence that makes mental and emotional trauma less likely. Of course, there's no perfect solution—soldiers who are trained in the principles of violence can still suffer emotional trauma, for instance—but it is no coincidence that the special forces operators who train the principles most rigorously, and end up having to use lethal violence most often, are the least likely by percentage to return to civilian life with crippling emotional distress.

There is a final piece to Bonnie's story that shines a light on this very fact. During her interview with the police officers on the scene in the immediate aftermath of her attack, one of the officers, seeing her therapy dog in the backseat of her car, asked Bonnie if she was licensed for a concealed carry weapon. She told him that she was and that the weapon was currently in her purse. The officers looked at her somewhat surprised.

"Why didn't you shoot him, ma'am?" They asked, curiously. "You would have been well within your rights."

"He was already nonfunctional," Bonnie told them calmly. "I determined there was no need."

Bonnie was now a two-time victim of asocial violence. When she came to us for training, she was fully in the clutches of PTSD from her first encounter—a brutal assault. It's not hard to imagine that a second attack might have sent her over the edge. She'd either freeze like a deer in headlights—*Not again, why me?!*—or go nuts and empty her pistol into her attacker's head, chest, and groin, before retreating inside herself like an emotionally broken zombie.

None of those things happened. Bonnie's knowledge of and training in violence stripped all the emotion and moral judgment out of it. Nothing that occurred in the Home Depot parking lot was a reflection on her inherent goodness or the unfairness of the world. It was the reality of an asocial predator meeting the reality of a prepared woman. I have spoken with Bonnie many times since her second attack, and she remains as mentally and emotionally strong as she is physically.

One person I haven't spoken to, for decades now, is a high school friend whom I'll call Efram. I haven't seen or heard from him since I got out of the Navy, since he killed a man.

Efram was a student of a Filipino martial art called Kali that focuses primarily on stick- and knife-fighting. When I knew him, he was already very good. One night he was out with his girlfriend in San Diego when a pair of armed men accosted them. It was unclear to Efram whether they were muggers, rapists, or what. All he knew was that one of them had a knife and the other had a gun.

With zero hesitation, Efram pulled his blade. Acting immediately, he knocked out the attacker with the knife, closed the distance on the attacker with the gun, disarmed him and, summoning all his martial arts training, carved out the man's throat. The attacker bled out right in front of them.

Strictly by the standards of physical training, Efram did everything right. He didn't hesitate. He acted first and fast. He put all his weight through both men, targeting vulnerable areas on their bodies that, when injured, produced an insurmountable spinal reflex reaction that took their brains out of the equation—knocking one out and killing the other.

But that was no consolation to Efram, because none of those objective facts could overcome the sound of gurgling coming from the dead man's throat and the sight of his eyes bulging from their sockets, blood pulsing rhythmically from his neck, and the life quickly leaving his body. Those sights and sounds haunted Efram and dogged him, no matter what he did to try to silence or escape them.

That's what his father told me, at least, when I ran into him one day in Mission Beach and asked him how Efram was doing. The whole thing really messed him up, Efram's father said. It had been five years and he still hadn't recovered. I didn't pry, but it was clear that drugs and alcohol had become a major part of Efram's coping mechanism.

So why did the justifiable use of violence in an inescapable life-or-death situation break Efram but strengthen Bonnie, someone who'd already suffered a traumatic attack? Of course, I imagine that part of the difference had to do with the fact that Efram took a life to protect himself, while Bonnie didn't have to. But I don't think that's all there is to it: a key difference was that Efram was only trained in the techniques of violence, not in their principles. He didn't know what the trauma he had trained to inflict would look like or sound like if he were ever in the position to inflict it, because that is not the end goal of most martial arts. He didn't know *why* the targets he struck were targets. No one ever taught him what an injury was from a physiological, anatomical perspective.

Bonnie knew all that stuff. She had studied and trained on the principles of the tool of violence, so that if she ever had to wield it she would know what to expect. By training slowly, deliberately, and repeatedly, she set her intent—inflicting debilitating injury to save her life—and she imagined what such an injury might look and feel like, just like we showed her in our training. She knew how her attacker was likely to move if she collapsed his trachea, and she understood the structural, anatomical damage she could inflict by shattering his knee. She didn't experience those things beforehand, but at least she was as prepared for them as it is possible to be—more prepared than Efram was.

That knowledge strengthened her mind as much as it strengthened her body. It left her *fully* prepared and, as such, completely at peace with herself, her choices, and her world.

CHAPTER TEN

IN THE END

I don't even call it violence when it's in self-defense; I call it intelligence.

—Malcolm X

You have a decision to make. There are no more excuses. Your brain is now equipped with information that could save your life.

Now you must decide whether you will put aside any discomfort or reservations you may have had about violence when you first opened this book, and allow all that you have learned to stick in your brain, code into your muscle memory, and marry to your soul. To me, it is a simple decision, though I recognize that it might not be an easy one for you, because you've learned *a lot,* which can make the choice appear more difficult.

You've learned some hard truths about violence. You've learned that violence is a tool—a weapon that does the same things in the hands of "bad guys" and "good guys." You've learned the facts that distinguish fantastical and competitive violence from the ugly realities of real violence in life-or-death situations. You can distinguish social aggression, the kind that happens within systems of rules and can usually be de-escalated, from asocial violence that can plunge you into a fight for your life.

You know that in a life-or-death situation, you don't have to be bigger, faster, or stronger to be the one left standing. You don't have to spend years training in combat sports or martial arts—because real violence isn't a competition. It's about being effective.

We've looked at the decision-making process, and at the mindset you need to protect yourself in an asocial confrontation: one focused on acting and seizing the initiative, not on defending and reacting. It's the difference between these mindsets—the ability to remain in Cause State and put your enemy into Effect State—that makes the difference between life or death in many situations.

We've seen the worst of the worst. I've given you firsthand accounts from corrections officers and gang members so we can better understand the tool of violence and the mindset of those who use it. I've explained how criminals think of violence pragmatically and ruthlessly, how they prioritize the intent to inflict injury above all else. I've shown how we can learn from their mindset and neutralize their advantage. Now you know what they know: that wielding the tool of violence means ignoring our differences as human beings and focusing on our similarities.

You know the similarity that matters most: that you can shut down the brain of any human being by inflicting debilitating injury on certain vulnerable targets of the body. You know that to do this you must commit all your body weight in one direction, toward, in, and through your target to create a tunnel of wreckage that triggers a spinal reflex reaction your attacker cannot control or overcome.

I haven't given you a step-by-step guide to inflicting injury on every target—there's no "kick here, punch there" in this book—because real life doesn't follow any step-by-step guide. Instead, I've given you principles that will work in any situation and give you your best possible shot at shutting down your enemy's command center before they shut down yours. I've stressed the single most important point when it comes to training and practicing using the tool of violence: work *slowly* on the fundamentals. And finally, I've explained how a few small, easy, and cheap steps can dramatically lower your chance of finding yourself in a violent encounter in the first place.

So, what's it going to be? Will you accept this knowledge into your life? Will you prepare to act if necessary, or will you rely on hope at all costs? It doesn't sound like I'm offering you a real choice, I realize. But *it is* a choice, and one you will be making in the next days and weeks as you process the information you've just consumed.

Just remember, this book is meant to help you *prevent* violence from ever entering your life and to *prepare* you for it in the unlikely event that it rears its ugly head. I can imagine some of you thinking to yourselves right now, "Jeez, Tim, paranoid much?" But preparing for asocial violence doesn't make you a paranoid person. Paranoia is a symptom of *lack* of preparation—it's the fear that there is a threat lurking around every corner, coupled with the insecurity that comes from uncertainty and ignorance. Men and women who are truly prepared don't have to be paranoid—they know how to identify real threats, and they know that the correct response to those threats is ingrained in their habits and training, ready to be activated when it's a matter of survival.

MAKE PEACE

It sounds strange to say that knowing how to tear people apart can bring you peace of mind. But that's just what it does. People who learn to use the tool of violence for self-protection tend to be calmer, more peaceful, and more at ease in the world. I've certainly experienced these benefits in my own journey. Over the years that I've studied self-protection, I've become a more peaceful person. I'm not peaceful because I'm fearful, but because I understand my priorities more clearly. I avoid the avoidable because I know it's not worth it. I'm the first one to apologize if I inadvertently bump into someone. I'm the first person to say "I'm sorry" if I offend someone. If someone insults me, I shrug it off, from a position of strength, not weakness. I won't be drawn into the kind of escalating insult competition that forms the basis for so much social confrontation and accidental death.

I don't do these things because I'm a saint: I do them because I don't have a fantasy version of violence in my head, because I've seen where real-world violence leads. At the same time, I'm also the first person to inflict an injury if my life is threatened. I've seen the very same combination of qualities in others who have learned to use the tool of violence, from special forces operators to my successful clients.

If you knew them like I do, you'd know that they are quick to end violent encounters, and just as quick to avoid them.

I earnestly believe that a world in which more of us understood violence, in which we took it seriously and not as an object of fantasy, would be a more peaceful world with more people leading better, happier lives. Understanding how violence works doesn't make you a more fearful or aggressive person, it gives you a gift: a sense of calm and confidence, empathy and humility.

Just a few days into writing this book, I was walking into a store, absorbed in my thoughts, when I saw a person in front of me, coming out of the door. I was not close enough to catch the door upon his exit but also too far to make holding it open obvious and easy. We were both caught in an awkward no-man's-land. I could speed up, but that would be kind of weird, too, as if I expected him to hold it for me. I saw the inner struggle on his face, which suddenly went calm as he stepped aside and stopped the door with his foot, waiting for me. I graciously accepted the gesture and thanked him.

It was a small moment with a person whom I will most likely never see again, but that small decision changed the trajectory of my mood, my day, and is still with me. That moment, and others like it, larger and smaller, is what we're here for: being kind when we don't have to be—because we have the capacity and the tools to be unkind when we need to be.

Real-world violence is life changing, but rare. And while I've focused on the first part of that equation, and what it means for preparedness, we can't forget the second part. Thankfully, the chances that any one person will use the tool of violence in self-protection are thin, but the opportunities to make peace, to be kinder than we may feel, are many and daily. The more I learn about our fragility—the fragility of *any* human body—the more I'm motivated to make peace wherever and whenever I can, to steer away from the ship-wrecking shoals of petty ego, suspicion, and fear and into deeper, calmer waters. I hope that you'll be moved in the same way.

And while I have taken precautions against the worst that humanity has to offer, it does me, and you, no good to spend the limited amount of time we've been given on this earth living our lives in fear. Maybe fear brought you to this book or to training in self-protection. That's fine. Use your train-ing to let go of that fear. Train until you're prepared for the unthinkable—and then let it go. Let it sink in. In the short term, my goal is to give as many people as possible that sense of preparedness. In the long term, my job is to ameliorate fear, to help free people from it as this practice has freed me.

If violence is the failure of everything we love, then every day free of it should be spent reinforcing the things that make life good. Look for those opportunities to make peace. Smile when you don't have to. Lend a hand or hold a door. Reach out to help when those opportunities for kindness unfold. Do it because you're strong, not because you're weak.

In a world where the person holding the door for a stranger is too often seen as a sucker, where kindness is equated with weakness, it is a refreshing thing to see the strong and capable make way and lend a hand. I didn't need that stranger to stop and hold the door for me. I would have thought no less of him had he let it go; in fact, I wouldn't have thought of him at all, ever again. And yet here I am moved by that infinitesimal act, inspired to write and share it with you.

This can be an ugly world that makes you question a lot of things about humanity. Making peace with those questions, I have found, is usually the answer...until it's not.

ACKNOWLEDGMENTS

Writing *When Violence Is the Answer* was only possible with the help and support so many people, more than I can attempt to completely list here.

Some of those people I'm not allowed to name, and I'm incredibly thankful for their support behind the scenes. They do amazing jobs in dangerous environments, and were extremely patient with my questions and extremely helpful with understanding just how violence works in some of the worst parts of our society. To them, I truly, truly thank them for their service and sharing their expertise.

For those I can name, I'm especially grateful for the following people:

First and foremost, my incredible wife, Sasha. She is a captain with the Las Vegas Metropolitan Police Department, a mother to my four children, an incredible wife and support system. Without her I never could have been able to write this book and have the time to really craft the information. She supported my travel, my extended interviews, and time away from the family. And she did so with a smile on her face, and with tremendous love. For that I'm eternally grateful to her.

Steven Pressfield, the amazing author of so many great books, like *Gates of Fire*, and, of course, *The War of Art*. Years ago Steve hosted me at his house in Malibu, took me to dinner, calmly listened to me while I told him of my exploits, and at the very end told me I had to write a book.

I protested that I didn't think people would be ready for this type of information, nor find it interesting. He stopped me right there and said, "Tim, I've been listening nonstop for the last four hours, and I find it fascinating…so write the book." To him, I say thank you. He's the only reason this book exists.

My good friend, Tony Robbins. He has been an amazing friend and supporter. Tony came and trained with me years ago, and our relationship has grown ever since. He made sure that I got the intros to the right people that allowed this book and others to be written. He's been a tireless supporter of mine, and for that I'm eternally grateful. It's rare when I meet a celebrity who truly walks the walk. Tony is that guy. Thank you, brother.

Officer Jason Seely, who works at Clark County Detention Center. Jason is a well-connected, low-profile operator in the corrections community, and he selflessly opened many doors to the asocial world of prison gangs, putting me in touch with subject-matter experts whom I never would have had access to as a civilian. They patiently answered my questions, and when it was understood what I was looking for, they thought it was unique and were very helpful. Without Jason this book wouldn't have much of the crucial info that is critical to true self protection. They shared so much great info; much that was beyond the scope of this book. That is my motivation to dig deeper into this world for my next book and share more of these useful yet disturbing truths.

My good friend and Master Instructor Chris Ranck-Buhr. Chris and I have been training people how to deal with violence for almost a quarter century now. I believe Chris is one of the greatest thinkers and communicators when it comes to how to correctly train people for this subject, and I'm eternally grateful to have been able to spend all these years collaborating with him and learning from him. He's an amazing individual and, I feel, one of the best communicators when it comes to how to survive asocial violence. Many of the ideas in this book were crafted during my numerous conversations with Chris over the years. He is a gracious man, and a deep thinker.

I am eternally grateful to the very patient, world-class wordsmith Nils Parker. He helped me pare down almost 2,000 pages of information and arrange it, edit it, and wordsmith it into a tight, well laid-out manuscript. I don't know where I'd be without his guidance.

Ryan Holiday and Brent Underwood of Brass Check. Ryan, in addition to becoming one of my new favorite authors (*Ego Is the Enemy,* Daily Stoic), is a great strategist and really helped me craft a compelling proposal and then fight for the spirit of the book as we went along the process. Brent has helped me to make sure I reach out to the right people the right way to share the book's message.

To the TFT instructor staff, clients, and all of my associates that I've had discussions with about these topics over the past twenty years. Much of what's in this book has been developed from those conversations and observations. I'm blessed to be surrounded by so many amazing people, who have delved into this topic with me. Luckily, I never have to worry about being the smartest person in the room, and I'm incredibly thankful for that fact.

To all the great folks at Little, Brown: my editor John Parsley, Gabriella Mongelli, and Michael Noon. They took me through every step of the process, were extremely patient with delays, and really supportive in putting out the book that I've wanted to put out for quite some time. I can't thank them all enough.

To Byrd Leavell, my amazing agent, who fought for this book, and fought for the tone of the book. He got me the deal, and was tireless in his support. I very much appreciate him. He's a fantastic guy, as well as an incredible agent.

Last but not least, I want to thank my children. My oldest, Conner, is in his twenties as I write this book. He was in my thought process the whole time I was writing it, hoping that he gets to navigate these years without having to use any of this information.

My three youngest, my son Brock and my twin daughters, Rumi and Raegan: It is truly my hope that they get to live lives free of asocial violence. I know that would be a very rare thing, so just in case, I'm leaving this book behind to help them navigate. They were my inspirations.

INDEX

ABOUT THE AUTHOR

Tim Larkin is one of the world's foremost experts on violence. As a former military intelligence officer, he was part of a beta group that redesigned how Special Operations personnel trained for close combat. Over the course of his twenty-five-year career, through his company, Target Focus Training (TFT), he has trained more than ten thousand people in more than fifty countries how to deal with imminent violence, including elite combat units, celebrities, and high-status executives, law enforcement agencies, and high-net-worth families. Larkin is also the author of the *New York Times* bestselling book *Survive the Unthinkable.* He lives in Las Vegas, Nevada.